access

EDWARD VI
and MARY:
A MID-TUDOR CRISIS?

Second Edition

Nigel Heard

Hodder & Stoughton

A MEMBER OF THE HODDER HEADLINE GROUP

Acknowlwdgements

The cover illustration shows a portrait of Mary Tudor by Moro, reproduced courtesy of AKG Photo, London.

The publishers would like to thank the following individuals, institutions and companies for permission to reproduce copyright illustrations in this book: Mary Evans Picture Library, page 10; Edward VI by an unknown artist/Katz Pictures Ltd/Mansell/Time Inc. page 33; Mary Evans Picture Library page 44; Edward VI and the Pope by an unknown artist/National Portrait Gallery, page 85; Martyrdom of Cranmer from Fox's Book of Martyrs, 1776/Mary Evans Picture Library, page 96.

Every effort has been made to trace and acknowledge ownership of copyright. The publishers will be glad to make suitable arrangements with any copyright holders whom it has not been possible to contact.

Orders: please contact Bookpoint Ltd, 78 Milton Park, Abingdon, Oxon OX14 4TD. Telephone: (44) 01235 827720, Fax: (44) 01235 400454. Lines are open from 9.00 - 6.00, Monday to Saturday, with a 24 hour message answering service. Email address: orders@bookpoint.co.uk

British Library Cataloguing in Publication Data

A catalogue record for this title is available from the British Library

ISBN 0 340 74317 4

First published 2000

Impression number	10	9	8	7	6	5	4	3	2	1
Year		2005	2004	2003	2002	2001	2000			

Typeset by Sempringham publishing services, Bedford.
Printed in Great Britain for Hodder & Stoughton Educational,
a division of Hodder Headline Plc, 338 Euston Road, London NW1 3BH
by Redwood Books, Trowbridge, Wilts.

Contents

Preface

To the general reader

Although the *Access to History* series has been designed with the needs of students studying the subject at higher examination levels very much in mind, it also has a great deal to offer the general reader. The main body of the text (i.e. ignoring the 'Study Guides' at the ends of chapters) forms a readable and yet stimulating survey of a coherent topic as studied by historians. However, each author's aim has not merely been to provide a clear explanation of what happened in the past (to interest and inform): it has also been assumed that most readers wish to be stimulated into thinking further about the topic and to form opinions of their own about the significance of the events that are described and discussed (to be challenged). Thus, although no prior knowledge of the topic is expected on the reader's part, she or he is treated as an intelligent and thinking person throughout. The author tends to share ideas and possibilities with the reader, rather than passing on numbers of so-called 'historical truths'.

To the student reader

Although advantage has been taken of the publication of a second edition to ensure the results of recent research are reflected in the text, the main alteration from the first edition is the inclusion of new features, and the modification of existing ones, aimed at assisting you in your study of the topic at AS level, A level and Higher. Two features are designed to assist you during your first reading of a chapter. The *'Points to Consider'* section following each chapter title is intended to focus your attention on the main theme(s) of the chapter, and the issues box following most section headings alerts you to the question or questions to be dealt with in the section. The *'Working on ...'* section at the end of each chapter suggests ways of gaining maximum benefit from the chapter.

There are many ways in which the series can be used by students studying History at a higher level. It will, therefore, be worthwhile thinking about your own study strategy before you start your work on this book. Obviously, your strategy will vary depending on the aim you have in mind, and the time for study that is available to you.

If, for example, you want to acquire a general overview of the topic in the shortest possible time, the following approach will probably be the most effective:

1. Read Chapter 1. As you do so, keep in mind the issues raised in the *'Points to Consider'* section.
2. Read the *'Points to Consider'* section at the beginning of Chapter 2 and decide whether it is necessary for you to read this chapter.

3. If it is, read the chapter, stopping at each heading or sub-heading to note down the main points that have been made. Often, the best way of doing this is to answer the question(s) posed in the Issues boxes.
4. Repeat stage 2 (and stage 3 where appropriate) for all the other chapters.

If, however, your aim is to gain a thorough grasp of the topic, taking however much time is necessary to do so, you may benefit from carrying out the same procedure with each chapter, as follows:

1. Read the chapter as fast as you can, and preferably at one sitting. As you do this, bear in mind any advice given in the *'Points to Consider'* section.
2. Study the flow diagram at the end of the chapter, ensuring that you understand the general 'shape' of what you have just read.
3. Read the *'Working on ...'* section and decide what further work you need to do on the chapter. In particularly important sections of the book, this is likely to involve reading the chapter a second time and stopping at each heading and sub-heading to think about (and probably to write a summary of) what you have just read.
4. Attempt the *'Source-based questions'* section. It will sometimes be sufficient to think through your answers, but additional understanding will often be gained by forcing yourself to write them down.

When you have finished the main chapters of the book, study the 'Further Reading' section and decide what additional reading (if any) you will do on the topic.

This book has been designed to help make your studies both enjoyable and successful. If you can think of ways in which this could have been done more effectively, please contact us. In the meantime, we hope that you will gain greatly from your study of History.

Keith Randell

1 A Crisis in Mid-Tudor England?

This chapter deals with the meanings which can be given to the term 'crisis'. In addition, the first section introduces some of the major political figures in the period 1547-58, and outlines the problems that they faced. By the time you have read the second section, on how historians' interpretations of events in mid-Tudor England have changed over time, you should be able to decide what is meant by the term 'crisis'. The remainder of the chapter should help you to identify and list the various types of problem or potential crisis in politics, foreign affairs, religion, society and the economy which mid-Tudor governments had to overcome.

1 Mid-Tudor England, 1547-58

> **KEY ISSUE** What was the political 'shape' of the mid-Tudor period in England?

Henry VIII's death in 1547 marked the beginning of eleven years of unstable government and this has prompted many historians to see it as a period of crisis.

a) Edward VI: the Somerset Years, 1547-49

Henry VIII was succeeded by nine year old prince Edward, his son by his third wife, Jane Seymour. This was a problem in itself because Edward was too young to rule, and periods of minority government were always times of potential political unrest. Henry VIII had tried to prevent trouble by establishing a Regency Council led by Edward Seymour, Edward's uncle. Edward Seymour quickly gained control of the Council, and, under his new title of Lord Proctector Somerset, (he had been made Duke of Somerset by his young nephew) ruled the country until 1549. During this time the political situation deteriorated steadily. One thing you need to decide is whether this was caused by Somerset's lack of ability, or by the numerous difficulties which he had to overcome.

Two major problems were inherited from the policies of Henry VIII. In 1531 Henry had made himself Supreme Head of the Church of England and had broken away from the Roman Catholic Church. Since then the ruling elites had been split over the issue of whether the English Church should remain essentially Catholic or become more Protestant. Somerset himself was a moderate reformer, as were most members of the Council, whereas Edward VI, despite his youth, favoured more radical changes. However, powerful politicians such as the Duke of Norfolk and Bishop Gardiner were opposed to change, and such differences only increased the in-fighting among the political factions. Somerset also inherited a war with France and Scotland through which Henry VIII had hoped to secure the marriage of Edward VI to the young Mary Queen of Scots. Although the government was already bankrupt, Somerset continued the war and thereby further crippled the country's finances. Apart from this, the English economy was in a very weak condition. Population levels had been rising rapidly since the 1530s, causing prices to rise and making it difficult for young people to find work. The problem was made worse by a fall in demand for English textiles abroad, which caused rising unemployment among cloth workers. By 1549 there was widespread discontent among the mass of the population, leading to large-scale popular uprisings in Norfolk and the West Country. Although the rebellions were eventually surpressed, Somerset's enemies on the Council seized the opportunity to over-throw him and take power.

b) Edward VI: the Northumberland Years, 1550-53

From the ensuing power struggle John Dudley, Earl of Warwick, emerged as the new leader. He was made Duke of Northumberland and Lord President of the Council. He ruled the country as the Lord President Northumberland for the remainder of Edward VI's reign. While Northumberland seems to have adopted more pragmatic poli-cies than Somerset you will need to decide whether he was any more successful in overcoming the problems that faced the country.

Although the popular discontent had been subdued, Northumberland faced the same problems as his predecessor. Somerset's fall had enabled the French to gain the initiative in the war, and lack of money forced Northumberland to make peace with both France and Scotland. This annoyed many of the elites who thought that this was a humiliating climb-down. At the same time, possibily to secure the support of Edward VI, he allowed increasingly radical reforms to be introduced into the Church of England. Such a move not only angered the Catholic elites, but also antagonised Emperor Charles V, England's major continental ally, who was an active supporter of the Roman Catholic Church. However, Northumberland had learned from Somerset's mistakes and intro-duced measures to try to restore stability. The Council and the government were reorganised, finances were reformed, and debts created by the war began to be paid off. Although the economic situ-ation continued to worsen, new poor laws were introduced to help the poorest sections of society. Whether Northumberland would have succeeded in establishing himself firmly in power is a matter of speculation because Edward VI died in 1553.

This created an immediate constitutional crisis. Under Henry VIII's will, Mary, the daughter of his first wife, Catherine of Aragon, was to succeed if Edward died childless. However, Mary was a devout Roman Catholic and it was feared that she would restore the authority of the Pope and so end the royal supremacy over the Church of England. In an effort to prevent this, Northumberland tried to change the succession by disinheriting Mary and her younger sister Elizabeth, the daughter of Henry VIII's second wife, Anne Boleyn. Instead, the Crown was to pass to Lady Jane Grey, the Protestant grandaughter of Henry VIII's sister Mary. Moreover, to secure his own position, Northumberland arranged for Lady Jane Grey to marry his son Guildford Dudley. The plot seemed to have succeeded and Jane was crowned Queen, but the elites of all religious persuasions rallied to the support of Mary. Whether through dislike of Northumberland, or to preserve the legitimate succession is not altogether clear. Northumberland was arrested, and eventually, he, Lady Jane Grey and Guilford Dudley were executed.

c) Mary Tudor, 1553-58

Until quite recently historians have dismissed Mary as being over-zealous in her support of Roman Catholicism and Spain, and lacking political experience and leadership qualities. Certainly, by the end of her reign her religious and overseas policies had made her widely unpopular. However, it is now suggested that her reign was not altogether disastrous, and that, but for her early death, her policies might have succeeded. You will need to decide which of these judgements is the more accurate.

Mary was widely popular on her accession and had the full support of Parliament. Her two major objectives were to return England to Roman Catholicism, and to create closer links with the Habsburgs, her mother's family headed by the Emperor Charles V. In the first year of her reign, Parliament agreed to annul all the Protestant legislation passed under Edward. However, before going further Mary needed to strengthen her position. To achieve this she proposed to marry Charles V's son Philip II of Spain. Although the Council and Parliament somewhat reluctantly agreed to the marriage, there was increasing opposition to the proposal. Many of the elites feared that England would be dominated by Spain and drawn into the Habsburg wars against France. An unsuccessful anti-Spanish rebellion in 1554 led by Sir Thomas Wyatt did nothing to ease such fears. With the Habsburg alliance secured, Mary began the task of restoring the Church of England to Roman Catholicism. Many of the elites had misgivings about such a policy. Some disliked the idea of the royal supremacy over the Church being ended, while others feared that they might have to return the Church lands which had been sold off to the elites during the reigns of Henry VIII and Edward VI. In the end Mary had to compromise, and although papal authority was restored, no attempt was made to reclaim any Church lands that had been sold. At the same time, the Marian government began another round of financial reform to reduce costs and increase revenues, and initiated a thorough review of the navy.

Before any benefits could be gained from these reforms the reign was overtaken by events. The persecution and execution of Protestants made Mary increasingly unpopular with all levels of society. Popular discontent was made worse by the steadily worsening economic situation and rising unenployment. Anti-Spanish feelings rose to fever pitch when Philip II, despite his promises to the contrary, involved England in his war with France and Calais, England's last continental possession, was lost to the French. Mary's death in 1558 was greeted with just as much enthusiasm as had been her accession five years earlier.

2 The Historiographical Background

> **KEY ISSUES** What is meant by the term 'mid-Tudor crisis'? In what ways have historians' views about the mid-Tudor crisis changed over the last hundred years?

a) The Whig Interpretation of History

Until the Second World War English historical writing was still largely dominated by the Whig interpretation of history. The middle of the sixteenth century was seen as a 'dead' period between the exciting changes under Henry VIII and the consolidation and expansion of the reign of Elizabeth I. This was because the Whig historians of the nineteenth century did not see any great or 'progressive' events taking place in England at this time. They therefore regarded the reigns of Edward VI and Mary as unimportant. Whig historians assumed that events were shaped by 'great' men (or women). This attitude has created the traditional view of the period, and the years between 1547 and 1558 have tended to be seen in terms of personalities rather than events. The major and tragic figures have been the dying boy king and the haunted, half-Spanish Mary, driven by love for Philip II and the Catholic religion to commit atrocities against her Protestant subjects. In the background lurked the obscure and slightly sinister figures of the Lord Protector Somerset and the Lord President Northumberland, one provoking popular rebellion and the other plotting to seize the Crown. These were the people who were thought to have created history and little attention was given to the mass of the population, or to the underlying issues which shaped events.

b) The Revisionist/Marxist Debate

During the 40 years following the end of the Second World War historians changed their views about the mid-sixteenth century. Much research was undertaken which showed that it was in fact a highly relevant period of development in English history. However, although it was agreed that the period was significant, there was no agreement about the way in which it was important. It was seen as a time of potential crisis, but there is a wide disparity of views over both the cause and the nature of any such crisis. There were two broad schools of thought – revisionist and Marxist. Not only were the two groups mutually opposed, but members of both schools disagreed among themselves. Revisionist interpretation largely concentrated on the short-term changes in the constitution, politics and foreign policy brought about by the ruling elites. In contrast, Marxist historians mainly saw developments in terms of long-term changes in the economy and society. Both schools saw England as part of momentous changes taking place throughout Western Europe. To explain these developments they created general theories into which they tried to fit the ever growing range of conflicting evidence. Of these theories the two with the greatest bearing on mid-Tudor England were those of the rise of the State and of crisis.

c) General Theories of the Rise of the State and of Crisis

It is particularly important to understand the basis of these theories and how they applied to England in the middle of the sixteenth century. The idea of crisis became very popular among historians in the 1970s. Most revisionist and Marxist historians used these theories to explain the various problems experienced by western European countries. There was the crisis of over-population in the fourteenth century, the crisis of feudalism in the fifteenth century, the religious crisis of the sixteenth century and the general crisis of the seventeenth century. However, it must be remembered that the so-called mid-sixteenth-century crisis was confined to England and did not form part of a general European crisis.

A major difficulty for the student trying to understand any theory of crisis is to decide what is meant by the term. By definition a crisis is a brief moment of danger. So how long can a crisis last – a few months, a year, or a number of years? In the latter case, it is possible to see the whole period from 1547 to 1558 as a crisis, but it might be more realistic to see years of particular danger – 1547, 1549 and 1553 – as the potential crisis points in England. Clearly this raises the question of what creates a crisis. It could be said that a crisis results from an immediate short-term problem such as a foreign invasion, a rebellion or a harvest failure. Equally it could be maintained that a crisis is created by a combination of long-term problems which together threaten the collapse of government or the State. The problems in England during the reigns of Edward VI and Mary combine all these possibilities. Yet, even so, it has to be decided whether the English State was in serious danger of collapse.

Even before trying to answer this question it is necessary to establish exactly what is meant by the sixteenth-century State. Revisionist and Marxist historians were generally agreed that the feudal crisis and chronic anarchy of the late Middle Ages enabled western European monarchs to gain power at the expense of the Church and the aristocracy. There is broad agreement that those monarchs who were able to take advantage of this situation increased their power and became the centrepiece of a new type of State. They achieved this by creating permanent central and local bureaucracies dependent on royal patronage, and by controlling military power. At the same time these monarchs had to maintain a balance between the various sections of their subjects by gaining their acceptance of the legitimacy of royal authority. The main difference in approach was that while the revisionists were more concerned with the political and constitutional developments within the State, Marxists stressed the economic role of the State in the growth of a capitalist system. Thus when historians of either school discussed the sixteenth-century State they were visualising it as the monarch and the permanent machinery of central and local government through which he or she and his or her advisers ran the country.

It was generally accepted that, within this broad framework, the states of western Europe were created and developed along different lines depending on their geographical, religious, social, political and economic background. Unlike 'absolutist' states on the continent where, theoretically, the monarch was above the law, had independent sources of taxation and controlled paid officials and mercenary armies, England was a constitutional monarchy. English monarchs were answerable to Parliament and had to rule through Statute law. At the same time they had to rely on the revenue from royal estates, and whatever money they could persuade Parliament to grant them. In turn this meant that they could rarely afford to keep a standing army of mercenaries and had to rely on the goodwill of the aristocracy and gentry to raise troops from among their tenants. Shortage of money also meant that they depended on these same land owners to act as an unpaid bureaucracy to run local government – as Justices of the Peace for instance. While this might seem to indicate that the English State was in a weaker position than its more authoritarian counterparts on the continent, some historians suggest that the other side of the coin was just as important: that the English taxpayer was getting government on the cheap and was therefore less likely to rebel.

Order was seen as the central problem for the sixteenth-century State. Monarchs had to raise money for the ever-increasing machinery of government needed to maintain peace and security, manage the economy and create social harmony. To achieve this they had to increase their revenue, but extra taxation was unpopular and likely to provoke rebellion, so leading to the collapse of government. English monarchs depended on the active support of the majority of landowners and the middle orders (described by Marxist historians as the 'bourgeoisie'), and on the passive obedience of the great mass of the population who had no share in the running of the country. Anything that upset this delicate balance could create a crisis for the English State, if not necessarily for the English people.

d) Potential Mid-Tudor Crises

In terms of these broad theories, the death of Henry VIII in 1547 was seen as presenting England with a whole series of potential crises. Although Henry had made careful provision for the succession of his young son Edward, the prospect of a minority posed a serious threat to the stability of the government, particularly as the factions at Court were deeply divided over religious issues. This certainly represented a potential crisis for the State, which might have led to civil war, or invasion by a foreign power to restore the Catholic religion. As well as these political and constitutional difficulties, England faced a number of long-term socio-economic problems. By the beginning of the sixteenth century the English population had begun to recover from the worst effects of the Black Death of 1349 and the subsequent plague cycle. Rising population forced up rents and food prices and made it difficult to find work, causing distress among the urban and rural poor. These difficulties were made worse in the middle of the century by the temporary decline of the English cloth trade which threw large numbers of people out of work. Popular unrest was increased by the rapidity of religious changes between 1547 and 1550, as many people felt that their old, traditional way of life was under threat. This was reflected in the growing tension between husbandmen and cottagers on the one side and yeomen and gentry on the other. The former felt that landowners and richer tenant farmers were using the commercial and religious situation to their own advantage. So by 1547 England seemed to be in a precarious position with possible conflict among the ruling elites, the threat of foreign invasion, a failing economy and rising popular discontent.

e) New Approaches

The collapse of the communist Soviet state in 1989 largely discredited the revolutionary basis of much Marxist historical analysis. This effectively took any remaining fire out of the long-running debate between revisionist and Marxist historians. In any case, most historians have become suspicious of general theories, particularly of crisis. They have come to the view that history should be seen in terms of separate crises occurring in individual countries or regions at different times without any common linkage or cause. Although this does not necessarily rule out a mid-Tudor crisis, the concept is now no longer fashionable. Continued research has led to a considerable revision of ideas about all aspects of the reigns of Edward and Mary. Far from a danger of collapse, mid-Tudor government is now considered to show considerable strength in overcoming a series of potentially damaging difficulties. Religious change is similarly seen as having been achieved with remarkably little disruption when compared with the continent. Although there was popular unrest this is thought to have been caused by economic stresses rather than any weakness on the part of the authorities. The major crisis point is now thought to have been the economy which suffered not only from government mishandling, but also from a whole range of long- and short-term problems.

These are the issues which will be examined in the following sections to see which, if any, of them constituted a 'mid-Tudor crisis'.

3 A Crisis of the State: Politics, Religion and Foreign Policy

> **KEY ISSUES** Were potential crises most likely to have arisen from problems over a) the constitution and administration, b) the succession, c) relationships with foreign powers, or d) religious changes?

After the death of Henry VIII, religion is seen as having an increasingly significant effect on politics, government and foreign policy. This means that you not only have to consider what problems were caused by different opinions over religion, but also how religious differences influenced politics, the succession and foreign policy.

a) The State

By the early sixteenth century the State was assuming greater responsibility for every aspect of life. In much of Europe government was becoming centralised in capital cities such as London, and growing numbers of civil servants were being employed to administer both central and local affairs. At the same time, the State was trying to take control in areas in which it had had little or no influence during the Middle Ages. As the administration grew in size, statesmen realised that they had to take more control of the economy to ensure that the country was creating the wealth needed to pay the cost of government. Consequently, the government began to pass legislation to try (often without success) to regulate the economy, and place restrictions on the way in which individual merchants and industrialists could operate. Many European countries, including Catholic ones, were deciding that religion was such a fundamental concern that it could no longer be left under the control of the Pope in Rome. In England the Henrician Reformation of the 1530s had made the monarch Head of the Church and given Parliament control of religious policy. This meant that religion had become part of the State's social policy, by which the government tried to maintain stability and cohesion. Yet, while the English State had gained great power and influence, it was becoming recognised that the government was responsible for the welfare of all the people in the country. Not only was the State expected to help the poor by taking over the charitable work previously carried out by the monasteries, but, also, to find employment for all the able-bodied.

This broad picture of the English State is widely accepted. Although it may appear very much like the creation of the twentieth-century historians using hindsight, it was precisely in these terms that the people of sixteenth-century England saw it as well. Commonwealth, or 'commonweal', the word used by contemporaries to describe the country, was a nationalistic and patriotic concept, but at the same time it contained the idea that the government was responsible for the welfare of all citizens, just as all citizens had the obligation to serve the State. This is well expressed by John Pym:

1   The form of government is that which doth actuate and dispose every
     member of a state to the common good; and as those parts give
     strength and ornament to the whole, so they receive from it again
     strength and protection in their several stations and degrees. If this
5   mutual relation and intercourse be broken, the whole frame will quickly
     be dissolved, and fall to pieces.

Although this was written in the 1620s, Pym is describing what he saw as the good and well-balanced Parliamentary constitution and government of the sixteenth century. Of course, this was an idealistic view of government and society, which only worked partially and for some of the time. The government found it difficult to see all the connections between different parts of the framework. Individuals at all levels of society, like modern historians, had their own biases and priorities. The sixteenth-century English State could only function with the consent of a majority of the people, and the art of government was to achieve as much as was practicable in the circumstances.

b) The Monarchy

Crucial to the delicate structure of checks and balances was the monarch. Although the State was growing in power and becoming more stable with the development of new offices of state and permanent civil servants, it was still dependent upon the personality of the king or queen. Much of the thinking behind the duties of the State was paternalistic. Just as a father was head of a family and was responsible for its well-being, so the monarch was to the nation. Equally, just as the father expected obedience from all members of the family, so the monarch expected unswerving loyalty from his subjects. The relationship between the monarch and his people and his place within the State is clearly shown in the Treason Act of 1547:

1   Nothing being more godly, more sure, more to be wished and desired, betwict a Prince the Supreme Head and Ruler and the subjects whose governor and head he is, than on the Prince's part great clemency and indulgency ... and on the subject's behalf that they should obey rather

5   for ... love of a king and prince, than for fear of his strait and severe laws; yet such times at some time cometh in the commonwealth that it is necessary and expedient for the repressing of the insolency and unruliness of men and for the forseeing and providing of remedies against rebellion ...

Here is another view of the State which is very similar to John Pym's idealistic picture of the sixteenth-century constitution. Edward VI, although only nine years old, is seen as the father of his people. It is a relationship based on mutual cooperation and love, but the King, like a father, has to punish his children if they become fractious. In mid-sixteenth-century England the King was seen in these paternalistic terms, and was regarded as the keystone of the constitution.

Edward VI and his Council, from a woodcut on the Title to the Acts of Parliament 1551.

c) The Succession

Such paternalistic attitudes meant that many members of the ruling elites thought the monarch should be male. Many continental countries recognised Salic Law, which excluded women from succession to the throne. Although England did not do this, there was no tradition of female monarchs. Henry VIII's anxiety to beget a male heir seems to suggest that he considered that a female heir presumptive would create dynastic weakness. When Edward VI died in 1553, the Lord President Northumberland tried to exclude the princesses Mary and Elizabeth from the throne because they were regarded as illegitimate, and, because as women, they might endanger the security of the State by marrying foreign princes (see page 43). Instead, he attempted to strengthen his own control over the Crown by replacing them with another woman, Lady Jane Grey, who was married to his eldest son. Although Northumberland was unsuccessful, it is clear that Mary, after she had overthrown him in 1553, was conscious that there was opposition to the idea of a female monarch, especially one who was unmarried. In 1554 Parliament passed an Act Concerning Regal Power which made it very clear that, within the English constitution, royal authority was 'invested either in male or female, and are and ought to be taken in one as in the other'. Some constitutional historians see this as a very significant piece of legislation, which, by removing doubts about the right of women to rule in England, prevented constitutional crises in the future. For other historians, however, the crucial point concerning the succession was not one of gender, but the question of age and ability.

It is widely agreed that if there was to be a constitutional crisis in mid-sixteenth-century England, it was likely to be caused by the succession of the nine-year-old prince Edward. There is little doubt that England in 1547 could have seen a return to the chaos of the feudal anarchy of the Wars of the Roses in the second half of the fifteenth century. That there was no real crisis in either 1547 or 1553 is seen to be the result of the loyalty and support of the majority of the population for the process of legitimacy and law. The fact that the succession of a minor in 1547 did not cause an immediate crisis does not lessen the potential gravity of the situation. Historians are in broad agreement that a central feature in the development of the State was the struggle for power among the ruling elites. In such circumstances a strong, adult monarch was needed to maintain control, and the accession of a nine-year-old minor clearly opened the way for ambitious men to attempt to gain power.

d) Factions and Power Struggles

The revisionist school saw this power struggle as taking two main forms. At the Court, the centre of government, the courtiers formed groups, or factions, which were constantly striving to gain royal favour. This is not considered to have been particularly dangerous, because factions are seen as a normal part of Tudor government. A much greater threat was thought to have been the rivalry between the 'court' and 'country' parties – although neither were political parties in the modern sense of the term. The 'court party' was seen as consisting of the members of the Privy Council, government officers and courtiers, all of whom held office and enjoyed royal patronage. The 'country party' was made up of those among the elites who did not hold office or enjoy royal favour, and generally lived on their estates in the countryside. Members of the 'country party' were considered to have resented the growth of the central bureaucracy because they thought it was sucking power and wealth into London at the expense of the provinces. This theory is now treated with caution. However, the hostility displayed towards Somerset and Northumberland by many of their fellow members of the elites is thought to have been part of this, or some similar process.

Marxist historians interpreted this struggle for power as part of the class conflict between the old aristocracy and the rising commercial and professional groupings drawn from town and country. It was once fashionable to describe this in terms of 'the rise of the middle class' – a conflict between the new, commercially-orientated smaller landowners, merchants and professional men, and the old military aristocracy for the control of central and local government. Now it is agreed that these distinctions are much less clear-cut, and that it is often difficult to show the difference between merchants, rising gentry, and the old aristocracy. Most Marxist historians came to agree that the conflict was between active reformers and conservatives, who were drawn equally from the ranks of the aristocracy and the new rising groups. This was seen as the beginning of a struggle for power between Protestant commercial interests and the conservative, Catholic forces of paternalism.

e) Foreign Policy

Most historians have considered foreign policy to be central to the political development of the State. It is generally agreed that the major problem for the early modern governments was to find fresh sources of revenue to meet their rising costs. Increased taxation was unpopular and might lead to rebellion, while borrowing, or debasement of the coinage, was equally dangerous and might result in bankruptcy or high inflation, which merely added to the cost of government. The alternative was for the State to adopt an aggressive foreign policy to acquire land, wealth and trade. Unfortunately, warfare was extremely expensive, particularly because of the rapid changes in military technology. As a result a country waging war, even a successful one, might bankrupt itself.

By the middle of the sixteenth century England was neither strong nor wealthy enough to compete with the great continental powers such as the Holy Roman Empire, or France. This meant that it was necessary for England to ally with one or other of her more powerful neighbours. Until 1559 western European foreign policy was dominated by the conflict between the Valois kings of France and the Habsburg rulers of the Empire and Spain. Several diplomatic considerations made it natural for the early Tudors to ally themselves with the Habsburgs. France had been England's national enemy throughout the Middle Ages. Henry VIII's marriage to Catherine of Aragon in 1509 linked England dynastically with Spain and the Empire. This alliance not only offered more protection against possible French aggression, but it was hoped it might also help the English kings to regain the territories lost to France during the Hundred Years' War. Another important consideration was that the Habsburgs ruled the Netherlands, the major industrial centre in northern Europe. As the English economy was dependent on the export of cloth to the Netherlands, it was essential to maintain good Anglo-Habsburg relations. Although the English Reformation of the 1530s soured connections with the Catholic lands and Spain, the Anglo-Habsburg alliance was maintained until the death of Mary in 1558.

These issues will be discussed in greater detail in Chapters 2, 3 and 4.

4 A Crisis of the State: Social, Religious and Economic Change

> **KEY ISSUE** Can social and religious changes be said to have turned serious economic problems into a real crisis?

It is widely agreed that fundamental structural changes were taking place in western Europe in the sixteenth century and that these changes were the result of the breakdown of the late medieval economy. Despite differing opinions over detail, it is generally thought that the underlying structural change taking place was a movement away from a self-sufficient rural economy towards a commercial market economy.

a) The Breakdown of the Rural Economy

Marxist historians saw the breakdown in terms of a 'feudal' crisis caused by a deterioration in the relationships between 'peasant' tenants and their landlords. This resulted in a change from a feudal 'mode of production' to a capitalist 'mode of production'. They argued that the feudal mode was a set of relationships which governed the medieval economy. Production was controlled by peasant farmers who not only grew food for consumption by their own families, but also had to grow a surplus to support the clergy and the military and administrative elites. This process was called 'surplus extraction' whereby the extra food was collected through taxes, tithes and rents. These great landlords, it was claimed, spent their income on luxury goods, warfare and castle-building, and as costs increased they had to raise rents, tithes and taxes – a process called 'extra surplus extraction'. As the landlords did not invest their money to improve the efficiency of their estates by improving the quality of their land or introducing new farming techniques, the soil became exhausted and the level of food production fell. By the end of the Middle Ages there was growing resentment among the tenants who were faced by falling crop yields and rising rents. They began to abandon their farms, to refuse to pay rents and to stage rebellions. Such 'peasant' resistance forced the great landlords to lease out their land in larger units to commercial farmers, and this resulted in more tenants being forced off the land to work for wages in agriculture and industry. This was the new and more exploitative 'mode of production', based on wages, which was spreading in England during the sixteenth century. In turn, this new form of economic relationship caused further resentment, leading to class conflict between the wage-earners and the commercial 'bourgeoisie' in both town and country.

While non-Marxist historians agreed that these changes took place, they accounted for them very differently and saw no evidence of class conflict. For them the late medieval economic breakdown came as a result of drastic changes in the level of the population. By the end of the thirteenth century the population growth during the Middle Ages had put great pressure on land and food supplies. This population pressure, combined with inefficient farming techniques, had led to soil exhaustion and a 'Malthusian' crisis – when population outstrips food production and results in famine. The Black Death solved this problem by reducing the population by about a third. Further outbreaks of bubonic plague maintained a high death rate, so that the population of England had been reduced from about six million in 1300 to about one and a half million by the middle of the fifteenth century. Such a drastic loss of population led to a deep recession which caused a sharp reduction in food prices and rents, but created a demand for labour. As a result, wages rose. While this was very advantageous to the husbandmen and wage labourers, it was disastrous for the great landowners, who lost income from rents and the sale of foodstuffs. Furthermore, they had great difficulty in finding tenants, especially as many of the cottage smallholders found it more profitable to leave their farms to work for wages. The great landowners were left with no alternative but to rent out all their land cheaply on long leases of up to 99 years to ambitious members of the gentry and prosperous husbandmen, or yeomen. When the population began to recover by 1500 a new group of commercially-oriented small landowners – the gentry and yeomen –

had emerged. They benefited from the rise in food prices and rent levels, while themselves enjoying low rents because of the long leases obtained in the fifteenth century. The great landowners could not profit from the upturn in the economy until the long leases ran out in the second part of the sixteenth century, while the husbandmen suffered from rising rents, and the wage-earners from increased food prices. The apparent consequence was the rise of this new commercial group at the expense of the great landowners, husbandmen and wage-earners. The lower orders, looking back on what for them was the 'golden age' of the fifteenth century, resented these changes, and this was to be a major cause of popular unrest during the sixteenth century.

b) Problems of Mid-Tudor Agriculture

These two long-term explanations of change (or some combination of them) are still widely accepted as the cause of fundamental structural shifts in England. By the middle of the sixteenth century the government was beginning to face severe economic problems. The population had risen to 2.3 million by the 1520s and had possibly increased to over 3 million by 1550. This necessitated feeding the extra people – a difficulty made worse because of the of the drift of the rural unemployed into the towns to find work. As the towns were dependent upon the countryside for food this created great problems for the urban authorities. Many historians consider that continued rural self-sufficiency, whereby many farmers only produced enough to feed themselves and their families, made the situation even more difficult. Not only were traditional methods of family farming inefficient, but the continued presence of large numbers of smallholders prevented their land from being farmed commercially. This can be seen as the basic crisis of mid-century English farming: commercial expansion being severely limited by traditional self-sufficiency. However, there is little evidence that commercial farming was very successful in increasing the levels of food production. Although some new methods were introduced and farming became more specialised – particularly near large towns such as London – up to about 1550, many of the gentry and yeomen were more interested in sheep farming in order to benefit from high wool prices. To improve efficiency and to increase production many commercially orientated landowners fenced off their land from the old open fields. This was the cause of most of the complaints about enclosure of land and the eviction of tenants, particularly when former arable land was converted to pasture. Yet it was necessary to create compact farms and to fence off the common land to bring it under cultivation if farming was to become more specialised and productive. Such was the dilemma facing the government, and by the late 1540s the growing shortage of foodstuffs showed that population was possibly again outstripping food supply. This position was made worse by a growing number of harvest failures – posing the threat of another Malthusian crisis.

c) Enclosure

Quite apart from the potential danger of widespread starvation, this situation can be interpreted as presenting a long-term social problem for the authorities. The government aimed to maintain social stability and order while, at the same time, accepting increased responsibility for poor relief and welfare. The government did not wish to see small-holders evicted or forced to leave the land because they would either drift into the towns or become vagrants, creating a possible source of riot and unrest. Enclosures were seen as the major cause of economic problems and social instability, and the government tried to pass laws against the practice. The difficulty was that Parliament, representing the landed interests, often blocked such legislation. Even when anti-enclosure laws were passed, the local magistrates (who were landowners themselves) frequently refused to enforce them. Consequently, not only did the State show itself to be incapable of taking effective action, but it antagonised the landowners by trying to prevent enclosure, and the lower orders by not preventing it.

d) Urban Problems and the Cloth Industry

Although in the sixteenth century most people lived on the land and depended on agriculture for a livelihood, an increasing minority of the people dwelt in towns and were employed in industry. Here again the government encountered severe difficulties. It is widely accepted that there was a potential urban crisis in the sixteenth century, which was heightened by a slump in cloth exports. Once again the long-term causes of this situation can be traced back to the late Middle Ages. Early medieval industry was carried out in the towns and was controlled by craft guilds. The largest industry was clothmaking but output was on a small scale: most of the goods manufactured were sold locally. The major international export was wool, which was sold mainly to the Netherlands and Italy. By the thirteenth century many merchants and industrialists were beginning to leave the towns because of restrictive guild regulations and the high cost of urban overheads. The result was the establishment of a commercial rural cloth industry, based on the 'putting-out' system. It produced large quantities of semi-manufactured cloth which were exported to the Netherlands for finishing and sale. The new industry, mainly based in East Anglia and the West Country, continued to expand during the recession of the fifteenth century. This encouraged landowners to convert arable land into sheep pasture to meet the ever-increasing demand for wool. The transfer of the cloth industry to the countryside caused problems for many towns, and these were made worse by the recession during the late Middle Ages. In addition, because of the very high urban death rate, towns were dependent upon migrants from the countryside to maintain, or increase, their population level. The sharp decline in national population during most of the fifteenth century reduced the flow of migrants, and many towns began to shrink in size.

When population levels began to recover about 1500, people who could not find work in the countryside drifted into the towns. Consequently, many towns were faced with a new problem of having too many migrants and were unable to feed, house, or employ them. In addition, the number of migrants increased because the country-based textile industry was facing growing competition from new types of cloth made on the continent. This meant that from the 1520s there were frequent slumps in demand, and many laid-off workers were forced to go to the nearest town to seek work. By 1550 the Antwerp market had begun to decline, causing widespread unemployment among English clothworkers. Other sources of work were scarce. Although many people were leaving the land and were available for employment in industry, there was little investment in towns to create new jobs. Consequently, the towns faced a very real crisis. The urban authorities had to contend with the problem of housing and feeding large numbers of unskilled migrants with little prospect of finding employment for them. By the mid-sixteenth century the government was threatened by rising discontent in both towns and countryside. The poor agricultural performance meant that the towns had great difficulty in feeding their rising populations and this created the threat of serious bread and unemployment riots. The situation was no better in the countryside. Discontent over enclosures and rising rents was increased by the loss of employment in the rural cloth industry on which many of the agricultural poor relied for subsistence. In these circumstances it is hardly surprising that the Lord Protector Somerset was confronted by widespread popular uprisings in 1549.

e) Overseas Trade

To a large extent these economic problems were outside the control of the mid-Tudor government. To meet the increasing cost of the administration and expand the national economy the English State needed to find new markets both in and beyond Europe to raise national wealth. The exploration carried out by Spain and Portugal in the fifteenth century is seen as part of this general process of State development. Yet while Spain and Portugal were gaining new markets, colonies and raw materials and France and the Empire were growing in strength, England was preoccupied with the Wars of the Roses.

Far from gaining new territories and trade, she lost all her continental markets apart from the Netherlands. Only the new western European nation states had enough power and wealth to develop oceanic trade and to establish colonies in the New World. Many historians see this process of developing long-distance, world trade as essential to the growth of the new, centralised states and the expansion of western capitalism based on the principle of economic growth. The opening up of the new sea routes to the Far East and America began to shift the economic centre of western Europe away from the Mediterranean and towards north-western Europe. This Atlantic economy was eventually to be dominated by France, Holland and England, while, despite their early colonial exploration and monopoly of the world trade, southern European countries such as Spain and Portugal increasingly became economic backwaters. Clearly, in order to overcome her economic problems England needed to participate in world trade to gain the raw materials and markets to stimulate demand and create new jobs. The first two Tudor monarchs, however, showed little interest in Atlantic trade. Henry VIII in particular was much more concerned with his continental ambitions. In any case, England at this stage could not afford to antagonise her Habsburg allies by breaking their monopoly of the American trade. Not until after 1550, with the decline of the Antwerp market, was the English government forced to show any serious interest in colonial exploration and the establishment of new markets.

f) Protestantism and the Expansion of Trade

The emergence of this new economic system is still seen by many historians as being linked with the development of Protestantism. It has been suggested that it was significant that the countries of north-western Europe which were to dominate world trade were all strongly influenced by Protestantism, and especially Calvinism, while the more economically backward countries were all Catholic. Consequently the conflicts between the countries of the Reformation and the Counter Reformation can be interpreted as economic wars just as much as wars of religion. The reason for this economic divergence is seen to be the result of different social structures in Protestant and Catholic countries. The Protestant work ethic, it is claimed, encouraged thrift, hard work and commercial enterprise, while the Catholic religion was opposed to money-making and competition. The result was the continuation of traditional, self-sufficient peasant economies in the Mediterranean countries, while more progressive social economies based on wage labour developed in north-west Europe. Although it is widely agreed that such explanations are too simplistic to be totally acceptable, they still play an important part in interpretations of western capitalism. In 1550 England was still a backward, off-shore European island and was not to take any significant part in world trade until the end of the sixteenth century. However, many historians accept that the economic and religious changes taking place laid the basis for England's political and economic dominance by the eighteenth century.

g) Social Change

The changes influencing the economy also had a considerable impact upon the structure of society. Medieval society has been described as a feudal pyramid. It was based upon the ownership of land, military service and peasant agriculture. At the top of the pyramid was the king, who was the largest landowner. The military elites were made up of the aristocracy and their families, who held land from the king, and the knights and their families, who held land from the aristocracy. Below them came the great mass of the peasantry, who worked the land and provided food and labour for the elites. The only groups outside this structure were the clergy and the small number of people who lived in towns. The economic developments of the late Middle Ages began to change this structure, but it was a very gradual process.

It is widely agreed that a highly significant shift among the elites was the rise of 'the gentry', the class of landowners socially just below the aristocracy. Revisionists linked this development with the expansion of the State. They considered that the gentry increased in numbers and power because of the growth in royal patronage and in the opportunities to hold government office. Other historians, particularly Marxists, saw the gentry rising at the expense of the aristocracy because of their greater ability and willingness to take advantage of commercial opportunities available after the breakdown of the medieval economy. It is difficult to choose between these two theories. What is certain is that there were more openings by the sixteenth century than during the Middle Ages for men of initiative to increase their power and wealth.

The gentry are seen as an expanding group ranked below the aristocracy and above the yeomen. They included younger sons from the aristocracy and the upper ranks of the yeomen, as well as wealthy merchants, lawyers and professional men from the towns. Many Marxist historians saw the English gentry as the rising, capitalistic 'bourgeoisie', which was in conflict with the aristocracy. This is a difficult argument to sustain because many gentry families were related to the aristocracy, and the ambition of successful gentry families was to join the ranks of the aristocracy. It is certainly true that the gentry, who were becoming increasingly educated through attending university and being trained in law, competed with the aristocracy for offices in central and local government. They are seen also as supplying the capitalistic drive needed to bring about economic expansion, but there is no real evidence to show that the gentry were more commercially motivated than many of the aristocracy. What can be said is that the elites in general benefited during the sixteenth century from rising prices, and the redistribution of monastic and other church lands. Only by the end of the century did the rising demand for land and titles begin to cause real competition among the elites. However, this process was only just beginning by the middle of the century, although there were already some significant developments taking place.

Equally significant changes were taking place among the non-elites. By the beginning of the sixteenth century, peasant society, as it was to be found in Scotland, Ireland and continental Europe, is considered to have been rapidly disappearing in England. The spread of commercialisation placed considerable restraints on the traditional village framework. The loose, and largely egalitarian, peasant society was being replaced by a more rigid structure. This consisted of yeomen (holding more than 60 acres), husbandmen (farming between 15 and 40 acres), and cottagers (who had a cottage and a small plot of land). The enclosure of open fields and commons in some areas meant that smallholdings were being absorbed into larger commercial farms. Loss of access to common land deprived poorer families of grazing rights for their animals and stopped them from collecting firewood or gathering wild fruit and other necessities. This meant that the way of life for the rural poor, where the centre of work for the family was the home and smallholding, was being eroded. Those people who could not find work as wage labourers on the large commercial farms run by the gentry, yeomen and husbandmen, or in local rural industry, were forced to move away from the village. Many migrated to the towns where they joined a growing urban proletariat dependent on wage labour. It must be stressed that changes were generally very slow, and varied widely across the country. A great many villages remained entirely unaltered. Only in the Midlands and around expanding towns, where commercial farming was profitable, were large numbers of people forced off the land. Even so, for a government anxious to maintain the *status quo* and the traditional village structure, this was not an ideal situation. In an attempt to stop people moving away from the villages the government tried to legislate against enclosure, which they thought was the main cause of depopulation. To stop people moving about the countryside, laws of increasing severity were passed against vagrancy. However, what the government failed to realise was that a rising population and the shortage of job opportunities were the real underlying causes of this problem. It was this situation, worsened by increasingly frequent food shortages, that was the major cause of popular discontent in mid sixteenth-century England.

h) Religious Change

Religious change is still seen by many historians as being very important in this economic and social restructuring. Support for the English Reformation by a large cross-section of the more commercially motivated aristocracy and gentry is interpreted as showing hostility towards the Roman Catholic Church. The break from Rome can be seen as the removal of the 'dead hand' of a Church which, by its opposition to commerce and competition, was slowing the pace of economic development. At the same time the enormous wealth and great territorial possessions of the Roman Church in England were perceived as unproductive. It is suggested that support from the elites for Henry VIII's religious policy was based on their desire to acquire confiscated church property, which they could use commercially to their own profit. Certainly the seizure and, after 1540, the sale of monastic lands, was the largest redistribution of property since the Norman Conquest of 1066 and enabled an expansion in the number of the land-owning elites. However, there is little evidence to show that the Catholic elites were any less eager to acquire church property, or were less commercially successful, than their Protestant counterparts. Consequently, while it is possible to say that the Reformation promoted commercial change, it is more difficult to maintain that it was brought about for commercial reasons.

The impact of religious change on the lower orders is equally difficult to define. Many among the rural population were opposed to Protestantism, seeing it as a threat to their traditional way of life. Others, especially in the towns, welcomed the ideas of the reformers on the natural rights of man, equality, and the re-distribution of church wealth. These different responses to Protestantism have been cited by many Marxist historians as evidence of the loss of solidarity among the lower orders and of the beginning of the breakdown of community values and mutual support. Protestantism is perceived as introducing more radical ideas into popular protest, or, at least, strengthening those that already existed. Although extreme radical groups among the lower orders in England were always to be a minority, they are seen as playing an important part in increasing social tensions and pressures. For them the Reformation marked the beginning of the millennium, the thousand year rule of Christ, when all men would be equal and there would be no more hardship, poverty and unemployment. Obviously such ideas were very attractive in a period of sharply rising prices, food shortages and a lack of job opportunities, and increased the possibility of popular riot and rebellion in years of particular hardship. This was clearly a dangerous situation, and fear of popular rebellion added to the stresses already being felt within society. Although many of these social, economic and religious changes were only beginning in England by 1550, they can be seen as posing very serious problems to the government and represented a potential crisis for the State.

These issues will be discussed in greater detail in Chapters 4, 5 and 6.

Working on Chapter I

This chapter is designed to help you understand what historians mean by the term mid-Tudor crisis. You should use the first section to construct a basic chronological framework which you can fill out as you work your way through the remainder of the book. The second section explains how the views of historians about mid-sixteenth-century England have changed, the difference of opinion between

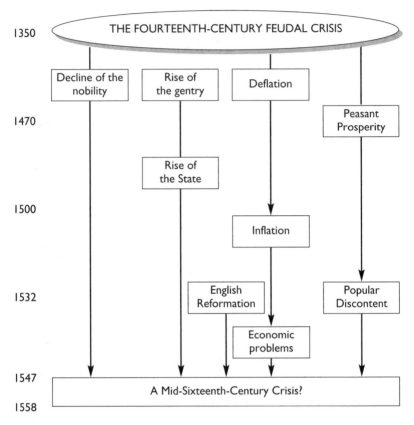

Summary Diagram
A Crisis in Mid-Tudor England?

schools of historians, and how they use the concepts of crisis and the development of the State to interpret events. You should note carefully all these changes of approach because you will need this interpretive framework to help you make sense of the events discussed in the other chapters of this book. Section 3 looks in more detail at the admininistrative, constitutional, diplomatic, political, and religious, problems. You should make a list of the major problems under these headings. Section 4 examines the problems created by social economic, and religious change and you should use these three headings to list the major problems that were created. The questions posed in the issues boxes will help you structure your notes. For both these sections your notes should show the differences between long- and short-term causes and how problems in one area could create difficulties elsewhere. At this point, you should make a provisional decision about whether any of the problems really amounted to a crisis. The following chapters deal with all these issues in more detail and will help you to come to a firm decision about whether there was a mid-Tudor crisis.

Answering structured and essay questions on Chapter I

In most examinations marks will only be awarded for answers which are relevant and clearly focused on the exact wording of the question. You will be expected to organise relevant information clearly and coherently, and to understand and to make use of the different approaches adopted by historians. Answers which are descriptive or just made up of a list of points will receive very little credit. Equally, answers which concentrate on one or two aspects and fail to cover the whole question will be penalised.

Therefore it is essential to read an examination paper carefully and to make sure you know what the questions are asking before attempting an answer. Examiners can ask questions about a topic in several ways, and each question requires you to organise you material in a way that is relevant to that question. It is essential that you identify the key words and make certain that you fully understand the meaning of a question before attempting to answer it. At the same time, to be sure that you have fully understood the meaning of a question, you should identify any assumptions, misleading or otherwise, that it contains.You will will gain very little credit for answering the question 'To what extent had the Church of England become more Protestant between 1547 and 1553?' by just making a list of the changes that had taken place. You need to think of the key words in a question, which in this case are – To what extent ... Church of England become more Protestant. An answer to this question requires a comparison between the degree of Protestantism in the Church of England in 1547 and in 1553, a knowledge of how and why changes took place, and an assessment of the extent to which the Church of England was more Protestant in 1553. On the other hand an answer to the question 'What religious changes had taken place within the Church of England between 1547 and 1553? (key words 'What changes' and 'within the Church of England') requires a detailed knowledge of the changes that took place between the two dates. A different approach is required to answer the question 'Why was the Church of England more Protestant in 1553 than 1547? (key words 'Why' and 'the Church of England more Protestant'). This question contains an assumption on the part of the examiners that the Church of England was in fact more Protestant in 1553, and part of your answer will be to test this assumption. As well as assessing the extent to which the Church of England was more Protestant in 1553 than in 1547, you will need to analyse the motivations of the major political leaders such as Somerset; Northumberland and Cranmer in making it more Protestant.

The same approach is needed for answering two-part questions, although at this level the examiners generally make it clearer what is required of you, and tell you the number of marks allocated to each part.

1. a) Outline the main religious changes within the Church of England between 1547 and 1553. *(12 marks)*
   b) Explain why the the Church of England had become more Protestant by 1553. *(18 marks)*

Notice the difference between parts a) and b). The first part requires you to know what the major changes were between 1547 and 1553, while the second part expects you to to be able to analyse the significance of the changes.

The great majority of questions set on this period will test your knowledge of the '3 "c"s' (causes, course and consequences), and your ability to apply your knowledge relevantly. Questions of this type fall into a variety of forms, but most follow a fairly standard pattern. The 'Answering structured and essay questions' sections at the end of Chapters 2-6 will be used to help you answer some of the types of questions most frequently used by examiners. You may well be expected to anwer a synoptic question for which you have to draw your material from a longer time span or a wider range of topics than usual. Advice on answering this type of question will be given at the end of Chapter 7.

Source-based questions on Chapter 1

As most examinations require you to tackle document questions, it is a good use of your time to practise answering the examples in this book. Remember that the documents have been chosen to test your ability to understand original sources, so that the meaning and significance may not be immediately clear. It will frequently be written in sixteenth century English and this will add to the difficulty of understanding the extract. This means that it is essential for you to read through a documentary extract several times until you are confident that you understant its meaning. Each question is allocated a number of marks and this indicates the number of relevant points that you are expected to make in answering it. This means that it would be pointless in spending more time on question 1d) below than on question 1b).

Attempt these questions to see if you can make enough points to earn the marks allocated. More advice on how to answer sourced based questions will be given at the end of Chapters 2–6.

1. The Nature of the State
Read the extracts from the writings of John Pym and from the Treason Act of 1547, given on pages 9 and 10. Answer the following questions:

a) Explain the meaning of **i)** 'the common good' in the first extract, and **ii)** 'commonwealth' in the second extract. *(2 marks)*

b) Both extracts describe what constitutes a well balanced State. What are the similarities and differences between the two descriptions? *(8 marks)*

c) What can be deduced from the extracts about the values and attitudes of the two authors? *(6 marks)*

d) How 'reactionary' or 'revolutionary' do the views expressed in the extracts seem to you? Explain your answer. *(4 marks)*

2. *Edward VI and his Privy Council, 1551*

Study the illustration of Edward VI and his Privy Council which is reproduced on page 10. Answer the following questions:

a) How old was Edward in 1551? *(1 mark)*

b) What were the probable aims of the artist in creating this picture? Comment in particular on the role of the monarchy. *(7 marks)*

c) How does the artist attempt to achieve his aims? Comment on the overall composition of the picture as well as referring to details within it. *(8 marks)*

d) How reliable is this illustration as a source of information about what happened at meetings of the Privy Council in 1551? Explain your answer. *(4 marks)*

2 Politics and the State

POINTS TO CONSIDER

This chapter deals mainly with four major areas of political problems which faced the three regimes governing England between 1547 and 1558. However, as you read the chapter you will encounter a wide range of problems – many more than four. Try to organise the problems you encounter into four groups. Give each group a name.

KEY DATES

1540-47		Last years of Henry VIII typified by factional rivalry
1547	Jan	Death of Henry VIII and accession of Edward VI
1547	Feb	Edward Seymour created Duke of Somerset and Lord Protector
1549		Rebellions in East Anglia and the West Country
	Oct	Fall of Somerset
1551		Emergence of John Dudley, Duke of Northumberland, as the most powerful man in England
1552	Jan	Execution of the Duke of Somerset
1553	May	Northumberland's son, Guildford, married Lady Jane Grey
	Jun	Edward VI changed line of succession
	Jul	Death of Edward VI, brief reign of Lady Jane Grey, and succession of Mary I
	Aug	Execution of the Duke of Northumberland
1554	Jan	Wyatt Rebellion
	Feb	Execution of Lady Jane Grey
	Jul	Marriage of Mary I and Philip of Spain
1558	Jan	Death of Mary I

1 Introduction

> **KEY ISSUES** Why is it often difficult for historians to interpret political history? How have they recently changed their views about the political situation in mid-Tudor England?

Political history is about a small elite of men and women who run the day-to-day affairs of a country. In trying to interpret events, political historians have to rely upon written evidence. State papers make it easy to discover what happened when. It is more difficult to find out why things happened. This is particularly true for the sixteenth century because many of the documents have been lost, or destroyed. However, lack of evidence is only part of the political historian's problem. Successful political leaders tend to manufacture their own history. Being in power they can create evidence which sets their actions in the best possible light. On the other hand, statesmen who fail are often unjustly condemned by those who replace them. The eleven years between 1547 and 1558 saw many such shifts in political power. It is for these reasons that political historians continue to re-assess their views about mid-Tudor statesmen.

Until the end of the Revisionist-Marxist debate historians generally accepted the interpretation that the mid-sixteenth century was a time of political conflict and confrontation in England– a period of failure and lack of progress, set between the great achievements of the 1530s and the recovery of the national economy under Elizabeth I. This was seen to stem from weak political leadership. The result was a contest between Crown and Parliament, and bitter strife between Catholics and Protestants. The three major political figures – the Dukes of Somerset and Northumberland and Queen Mary – have been blamed for this failure for various reasons. The 'good Duke' of Somerset was seen as a moderate reformer, who fell from power because of his tolerant and humanitarian policies. The Duke of Northumberland was considered ruthless and greedy, creating a constitutional crisis by trying to change the succession. Mary was condemned as inept for her obsession with Philip II of Spain and her devotion to Catholicism. General theories of crisis and the rise of the State only strengthened the opinion that the mid-Tudor period was one of failure and crisis. However, new evidence and research has caused these views to be questioned and revised.

The idea of a mid-Tudor political crisis is no longer popular. Considerable reservations are felt about the theories of the State and the Tudor revolution in government. Although there were disruptions, the machinery of government continued to operate normally. The period 1547-48 is now seen in terms of constructive debate and co-operation rather than conflict – as a time of definite political and administrative development. In part this change results from revised opinions about the political leaders. The Duke of Somerset is now seen as a typical Tudor soldier and statesman who was more interested in war than humanitarian reform. While the Duke of Northumberland is still regarded as ruthless and self-seeking, he is becoming recognised as an able and reforming administrator. Although no one has claimed that Mary was a great queen, her reign is being seen as a time of significant political and administrative progress.

2 The Last Years of Henry VIII, 1540-47

KEY ISSUES What was a) the nature and b) the significance of the political rivalry which existed during the last years of Henry VIII's reign? What was the political situation at the time of Henry's death?

In 1540 the fall of Thomas Cromwell, Henry VIII's chief adviser in the 1530s, heralded a period of increased political instability. There was a growth in the rivalry between factions at Court. The main issue lay between the parties supporting reform in politics and religion, and those 'conservatives' who wished to see less reform. Some 'conservatives' wanted there to be a return to Catholicism. The reform party was led by Archbishop Cranmer and Edward Seymour, later Duke of Somerset, the uncle of Prince Edward. The conservatives were headed by Thomas Howard, Duke of Norfolk, and Stephen Gardiner, Bishop of Winchester. The disgrace of Cromwell had been a success for the conservative party. It was confirmed by Henry VIII's marriage to Catherine Howard, the Duke of Norfolk's niece. However, Catherine's trial and execution for adultery in 1542 marked a victory for the reform party. For the next five years the two factions strove for supremacy at Court. Henry VIII's final marriage, to Catherine Parr, a committed Protestant, showed that the conservatives were losing ground. In 1546 the reformers gained a decisive advantage when the Duke of Norfolk was arrested and put in the Tower of London on a charge of treason, and Stephen Gardiner was dismissed from the Privy Council. It was against this background that Edward VI, brought up as a Protestant, came to the throne in 1547. Some historians see these disputes between the factions as a sign of increasing dynastic weakness. Others argue that factions were a normal part of Tudor politics, and that such rivalry was necessary for healthy government.

a) The Issue of the Succession

Apart from the wars with Scotland and France which had begun in 1542 and 1544, Henry VIII's major concern in his last years was the succession. Since 1527 he had been obsessed with the need to safeguard the dynasty by leaving a male heir to succeed him. The birth of Prince Edward in 1537 had seemed to achieve this objective. By 1546 the King's declining health made it clear that his son would come to the throne as a minor. To avoid any possible disputes Henry made a final settlement of the succession in his Will of 1546. This replaced the Succession Acts of 1534, 1536 and 1544, although the terms of the Will were similar to the Act of 1544. In the event of Edward dying without heirs, the succession was to pass first to Mary, the daughter of Catherine of Aragon. If Mary died without heirs her sister Elizabeth, daughter of Anne Boleyn, was to succeed. The major change to the previous settlement was that if all Henry's children were to die without heirs, the throne was to pass to his niece Frances Grey. Lady Frances was the elder daughter of Henry VIII's sister Mary, who first had married King Louis XII of France and then Charles Brandon, Duke of Suffolk. This clause meant that the other possible claimant to the English throne, the infant Mary Queen of Scots, was excluded. Mary was the descendant of Henry VIII's sister Margaret, who had

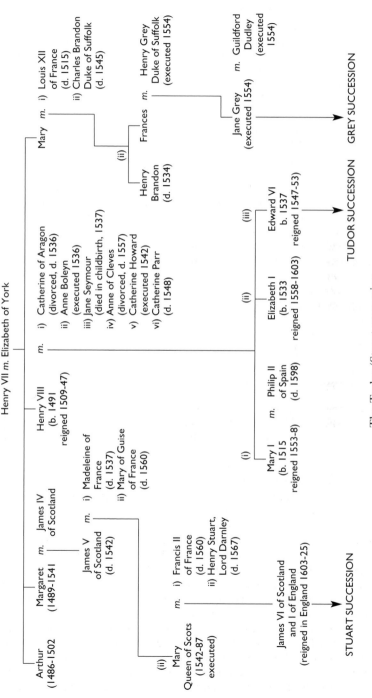

The Tudor/Stuart succession

married James IV of Scotland (see page 29). Henry was anxious to
preserve the royal supremacy, hence the inclusion of the Protestant
Grey family and the exclusion of the Catholic Stewart dynasty.
Although the Will had replaced the earlier succession settlements, the
Acts of 1534 and 1536, which had made Mary and Elizabeth illegiti-
mate, were not repealed.

Henry's major concern in his Will was to secure the peaceful succession of his son and safeguard the royal supremacy. By 1546 it had
become clear that the surest way to achieve this, and to prevent any
power struggle, was to give authority to Seymour and the reform
faction. The disgrace of Howard and Gardiner had secured the position of Seymour and his adherents, and this was strengthened by
adjustments to the terms of the Will right up to the time of Henry
VIII's death. A Regency Council was nominated consisting of
Seymour and 15 of his most trusted allies. Members of the Council
were to have equal powers, and were to govern the country until
Edward reached 18 years of age. In order to secure the loyalty and co-
operation of the Council its members were to be rewarded with new
titles, and lands taken from the monasteries and the Howard family.

3 The Protector Somerset, 1547-49

> **KEY ISSUES** Why was the Duke of Somerset able to rise to power so
> rapidly? What were his aims while he was in power? Why did he fall
> from power?

a) Rise to Power

In spite of Henry's precautions, it soon became apparent that the
plans for the regency were not practical. Even if there had been no
tensions between the conservative and reform parties, it is doubtful
whether a Regency Council made up of 16 equal members could have
operated successfully. The Council system of government in England
was designed to function with a chief executive, the monarch, to
make final decisions. For the Regency Council to operate successfully
it was necessary for one of its members to act as chief executive.
Edward Seymour quickly emerged as the leader of the Council. He
had been high in favour during the last part of Henry VIII's reign and
this, coupled with the reputation that he had earned through his
successful campaigns in the Scottish war, placed him in a very strong
position. He and his ally and fellow councillor, Sir William Paget, had
custody of Henry VIII's Will. They kept the King's death secret for
four days. This gave them time to take advantage of the weakness of
the conservative party and to rally support among the reformers and
moderates for the nomination of Seymour as leader of the Council.
The reason why Seymour gained power so quickly is not altogether

clear, although his being the new King's uncle certainly helped. Clearly the reformers among the clergy hoped for the introduction of religious reform, and it is likely that many moderates regarded Seymour as the best means of preserving stability and the royal supremacy.

Henry's death and the terms of the Will were made known to an assembly of nobles and higher clergy at the Tower of London on 1 February. At the same time Lord Wriothesley, the Chancellor and new head of the conservative party, announced that Edward Seymour had been made leader of the Council for 'the better conduct of business'. By the end of February Seymour had secured the firm support of the majority of councillors and was made Lord Protector, with the right to appoint and dismiss members of the Privy Council. These powers made Seymour the undisputed ruler of the country. He was created Duke of Somerset and was given confiscated monastic property to support his new titles. Other members of the Council were given new titles and estates, roughly along the lines laid out in Henry VIII's Will.

Somerset's success in reaching supreme power is often attributed to the support of the very able Paget. Therefore, any valid judgements about Somerset's character and capability have to be based on his achievements, or lack of them, over the ensuing two years if they are to be valid. There are three main views about his character. In the past he has been regarded as a genuine humanitarian, sympathetic to the plight of the poor. More recently, doubts have been expressed about whether he had any interest in social reform and it has been claimed that he was an arrogant self-seeker who refused to accept advice, and who enriched himself with confiscated church property. Using the same evidence, historians currently see him as a typical Tudor soldier and statesman, whose main interest was the war against Scotland and France. As such he is regarded as being no more greedy, and no more sympathetic to the poor, than his fellow aristocrats. Certainly in February 1547 the other members of the Council were just as quick to accept lands and titles as Somerset himself.

b) System of Government

Somerset took over a form of administration that had been developed by Henry VII and Henry VIII. Tudor government rested on the principle that the power of the monarch was based in Parliament. Both Houses of Parliament had to approve proposals for taxation and confirm any new laws before they became permanent statutes. On the other hand, the monarch could call Parliament to meet as often, or as infrequently, as he chose. When Parliament was not in session the Crown could make new laws through proclamations, or could suspend existing laws, but these actions had to be confirmed when Parliament met again. Certain things such as diplomacy and the making of war or peace were part of the royal prerogative, over which the monarch had complete control. Religion had always been considered part of the royal prerogative until Henry VIII used Parliament to carry through the English Reformation. Under Mary, and later Elizabeth I, religion was to become a matter of dispute between Crown and Parliament.

The day-to-day administration was carried out by the Privy Council. Members of the Council were chosen by the monarch from among the nobles, higher clergy and more important gentry. They were selected for their loyalty and their administrative or military skills, and could be dismissed at will. The work of the Privy Council was supported by a staff of permanent civil servants chosen mainly from the gentry, lawyers and minor clergy. The Privy Council was responsible also for the running of local government, with the support of the nobles, higher clergy and gentry. The two parts of the country which were thought most open to rebellion or invasion, Wales and the Scottish border, were administered by the Councils of Wales and of the North. These were regarded as sub-committees of the Privy Council, and were run by members of the local elites chosen by the Privy Council in London. Local government in the remainder of England was administered by the nobles and higher clergy in each county. They were expected to maintain order, administer justice, collect taxes, raise troops, and carry out instructions from the Privy Council. These duties had to be organised through their own households, and frequently at their own expense. In turn they were supported by the local gentry, who, among other things, acted as Justices of the Peace and commissioners for collecting taxes and mustering the county militias. The major problem with this system was that if the leading local families did not support the government, or did not like the legislation, they often failed to carry out instructions from London. This meant that the central administration had to be careful to maintain the confidence and support of the majority of the landed elites.

There is little evidence to suggest that the administration during the first two years of Edward VI's reign was markedly different from that of the last years of Henry VIII. The Privy Council was made up of men who had risen to power under Henry VIII and who were using the same methods and machinery of government to cope with similar problems. The real differences were the lack of effective leadership, and the fact that existing problems had grown worse. Economic and financial expedients and a half-hearted religious reform policy only created confusion and uncertainty among both the landed elites and the general public. It has been suggested that Somerset was neither more nor less to blame than his aristocratic colleagues. But whether this was because he was unwilling, or unable, to change their attitudes is uncertain. While there is no evidence that he tried to corrupt the government, it is equally true that he introduced no reforms. What can be said is that he failed to show the leadership necessary to compensate for the absence of an adult monarch. Whether this was because of his preoccupation with the war effort, or because of his stubbornness and inability to adjust to new conditions is difficult to judge. Some evidence exists to support each interpretation, but it is not conclusive.

Edward VI c 1546.

i) Short-term Problems

The new regime inherited three pressing short-term problems from the previous reign. Immediate decisions had to be made about whether or not to continue the wars against Scotland and France, about the question of religious reform, and about how to find ways of raising more revenue.

Whether or not Somerset's main interest was to bring the war to a successful conclusion, its continuation (see Chapter 3) was seen as a matter of national pride by most of the aristocracy and gentry. Consequently, any move to end the war would have lost him support among the landed elites. In any case, the Council was bound by Henry VIII's last wishes to arrange a marriage between Edward VI and the infant Mary Queen of Scots to secure the succession. This meant continuing a war based on the ill-founded belief that a military victory would force the Scots to agree to the marriage.

In 1539 Henry VIII had tried to prevent any further religious changes by the Act of Six Articles, which had laid down doctrines and forms of worship for the Church of England. Since then pressure had been mounting among the Protestant clergy and laity for the introduction of reforms along the lines of Lutheranism and Calvinism on the continent. Although the Privy Council was made up mainly of moderates, it was anxious to keep the support of influential reformers such as Bishops Ridley and Latimer. For this reason the administration had to make some gesture towards introducing religious reform if it was not to risk losing the support of the Protestant activists and encourage a Catholic revival, which might well have resulted in it losing power.

Revenue was the most pressing problem. In 1547 the government was virtually bankrupt. The crippling cost of the war was the main reason for this. By 1546 Henry VIII had already spent £2,100,000 on the war, and borrowed a further £152,000 from continental bankers. To pay for this he had sold off most of the monastic lands seized between 1538 and 1540, as well as some crown lands. By 1547 the annual revenue from crown lands had fallen to £200,000. This was insufficient to run the country and pay off government borrowing, let alone finance the war. There was an urgent need to reform the taxation and customs systems, and to bring the way that finances were administered up to date. Somerset and the Council, possibly because of their preoccupation with the war, did none of these things. Instead, they fell back on the old expedients of seizing more church property and debasing the coinage (see page 37).

ii) Long-term Problems

As well as these immediate political and administrative difficulties, the government faced a number of serious long-term economic and social problems. Population continued to increase, and this presented a major threat to the government. Increasing population was the main cause of inflation because greater demand for goods pushed up prices. Not only did this add to the cost of administration, but it also threatened most people's living standards at a time when wages were not increasing. In addition, it meant that more people were available for employment. This, in turn, caused more poverty because it also raised the number of vagrants looking for work. Fortunately, a run of good harvests kept the price of grain stable until 1549. Then a poor harvest made the the situation worse, and the level of popular discontent rose (see Chapters 5 and 6). The root causes of these problems were largely beyond the government's control, but continuing high levels of taxation and debasement of the coinage only made the economic situation worse. The main objective of domestic policy appears to have been the prevention of public disorder (see page 37), which the ruling elites regarded as a threat to the whole structure of society.

Therefore, Somerset and the Privy Council were faced with a considerable dilemma. They had to continue the war for the sake of national prestige and to retain the support of a large section of the elites. If they maintained the war effort the country would be plunged further into debt. However, if they raised taxes this would be unpopular with the elites and other taxpayers. At the same time they had to take some action over religious reform if they were not to lose the support of the Protestant activists. Such a loss of support might allow a Catholic revival which would endanger their hold on power. Yet if they went too far the reformers might provoke the Catholics into open rebellion. The administration was well aware that there was rising popular discontent over the worsening economic conditions. They feared that this might lead to popular uprisings, but they were uncertain how to tackle the economic problems. Therefore, whatever action the government took it was likely to cause as many problems as it solved. In the event, it appears from its actions over the next two years that the government's main objective was to continue the wars. At the same time it cautiously introduced some religious reforms and tried to damp down popular discontent.

c) Laws and Proclamations, 1547-48

When the government had established itself in power and decided its legislative programme, Parliament was summoned to meet in November 1547. One of its first actions was to pass a new Treason Act. This repealed the old heresy, treason and censorship laws and the Act of Six Articles which had maintained doctrinal orthodoxy since 1539. The removal of the heresy laws allowed people to discuss religion freely without fear of arrest, while the ending of censorship on printing and publishing enabled the circulation of books and pamphlets on religion, and the importation of Lutheran and Calvinist felt that the fencing-off of common land for sheep pasture and the consequent eviction of husbandmen and cottagers from their homes was the major cause of inflation and unemployment. Proclamations were issued against enclosures, and commissioners were sent out to investigate abuses. The main effect of these measures was to increase unrest. Hopes were raised among the masses that the government would take some decisive action, which it did not. At the same time, fear grew among the landed elites that the authorities would actually prevent this form of estate improvement. Further measures limiting the size of leaseholds and placing a tax on wool only made the situation worse by increasing these fears. In any case, many of the elites evaded the legislation which, consequently, fell most heavily on the poorer sections of society it was supposed to protect.

It reasonable to suggest that the government was more concerned with avoiding riot and rebellion than with helping the poor and solving economic problems. This suspicion is supported by three proclamations issued in 1548 aimed specifically at maintaining law and order. A ban on football was rigorously enforced on the grounds that games usually ended in riots and disorder. It also became an offence to spread rumours, as they were likely to create unrest. Finally, all unlawful assemblies were forbidden. Anyone found guilty of these offences was to be sent for varying periods to the galleys – royal warships propelled by oars. These seem like emergency measures passed by a government which realised that the economic position was getting out of hand, and which feared the consequences.

d) Fall from Power

It appears that these attempts to control the situation were ineffective because in 1549 the country drifted into what was potentially a major crisis. Somerset seemed unable, or unwilling, to take decisive action to suppress well-supported popular uprisings in the West Country and East Anglia (see Chapters 4 and 6). His unwillingness to act has traditionally been interpreted as showing sympathy. However, it seems more likely that the initial delays were caused by the reluctance of the local elites to intervene without government support. Lack of money made it difficult to raise a new mercenary army, and Somerset, as Commander-in-Chief, was reluctant to withdraw troops from his garrisons in Scotland and France. It was only when the Privy Council realised the seriousness of the situation and provided additional troops that Lord Russell in the West Country and John Dudley, Earl of Warwick, in East Anglia were able to defeat the rebels. A major consequence of the rebellions was the fall of Somerset, whose colleagues quickly abandoned him as a man who had failed to prevent anarchy and revolution. When his chief rival, John Dudley(later to become Duke of Northumberland, and hereafter called Northumberland to avoid confusion), fresh from his victory in Norfolk, engineered Somerset's arrest in October 1549 there was no opposition. Although Somerset was released early the following year and rejoined the Privy Council, within a year he was accused of plotting against the government. He was executed in January 1552.

4 The Lord President Northumberland, 1550-53

> **KEY ISSUES** What were the similarities and differences between Somerset and Northumberland as rulers of England? To what extent can Northumberland be seen as a skilful politician and administrator rather than just a ruthless power seeker?

a) Rise, 1549-51

Even before his arrest it was clear that Somerset was discredited and had lost control of the political situation. Many members of the Privy Council were offended by his aloofness and his arrogance in using his own household instead of the Council to conduct business. He had undermined the confidence of the aristocracy and the gentry because of his inept handling of the popular uprisings, while his religious reforms (see Chapter 4) had alienated even moderates among the conservative party. A power struggle soon developed in which Northumberland was a leading contender. Northumberland crushed the rebel army in Norfolk on 26 August and returned to London on 14 September. This gave him a distinct advantage because as the commander of the main army in England he controlled the capital. Almost immediately he began to negotiate with Lords Arundel and Wriothesley, leaders of the conservative party. In desperation, on 30 September, Somerset issued a proclamation ordering all troops in England to return to their duties in Scotland and France. On 5 October he issued another proclamation for a general array of loyal troops for the defence of the realm. There was no response, and Somerset removed the Royal Household from Hampton Court to Windsor Castle for security. Meanwhile the Privy Council protected its own position by issuing a proclamation blaming Somerset for the rebellions. All parties were anxious to avoid civil war. On 8 October Somerset agreed to negotiate on honourable terms, and was arrested three days later.

Northumberland, like Somerset, had risen to political prominence during the last years of Henry VIII's reign. He, too, had gained a good military reputation in the Scottish and French wars. He was a member of the Council named in Henry's Will and was ambitious for more power. The events of 1549 gave him his opportunity to take advantage of Somerset's political isolation. By mid-September he had emerged as the major rival for power, and had contrived to have Somerset childless. Mary's strong Catholic sympathies made her unpopular with the reform party and with Edward himself. Moreover, it was feared that Mary might renounce the royal supremacy. To prevent a return to Catholicism, and to retain power, Northumberland, with the full support of the King, planned to change the succession. As the Succession Acts of 1534 and 1536 making Mary and Elizabeth illegitimate had not been repealed, it was decided to disinherit them in favour of the Suffolk branch of the family. Frances, Duchess of Suffolk, was excluded as her age made it unlikely that she would have

Mary I, 1544.

male heirs and her eldest daughter, Lady Jane Grey, was chosen to succeed. To secure his own position Northumberland married his eldest son, Guildford Dudley, to Jane in May 1553.

Unfortunately for Northumberland, Edward VI died in July before the plans for the seizure of power could be completed. Jane Grey was proclaimed Queen by Northumberland and the Council in London, while Mary proclaimed herself Queen at Framlingham Castle in Suffolk. Northumberland's mistake was to underestimate the amount of support for Mary in the country. On 14 July he marched into Suffolk with an army of 2,000 men, but his troops deserted him. The Privy Council in London hastily changed sides and proclaimed Mary as Queen. Northumberland was arrested in Cambridge, tried, and was executed on 22 August in spite of his renunciation of Protestantism. The ease with which Mary upheld her right to the throne shows the growing stability of the State and the nation. Potential political crisis had been avoided because the majority of the nation supported the rule of law and rightful succession. The direct line of descent was still considered legitimate in spite of Acts of Parliament to the contrary. A period of dynastic weakness and minority rule had passed without the country dissolving into civil war.

Two Acts were passed, one in 1553 and another in 1554, to resolve the constitutional position. This legislation was designed to confirm Mary Tudor's legitimacy, and to establish the right of female monarchs to rule in England. However, no attempt was made to make

---

An Act Declaring Mary I Legitimate, 1553

1 ... in any other act or acts of Parliament, as whereby your Highness is named or declared to be illegitimate, or the said marriage between the said King your father and the said Queen your mother is declared to be against the word of God or by any means unlawful, 5 shall be repealed, and void and of no force nor effect, to all intents, constructions, and purposes, as if the same sentence or acts of Parliament had never been made ...

An Act concerning the Regal Power, 1554

10 For the avoiding and clear extinguishment of which said error or doubt, [that female monarchs could not reign in England] and for a plain declaration of the laws of this realm in that behalf; be it declared and enacted by the authority of this present Parliament, that the law of this realm is and ever hath been and ought to be 15 understood, that the kingly or regal office of the realm, and all dignities, prerogative, royal power, pre-eminences, privileges, authorities, and jurisdictions thereunto annexed, united, or belonging, being invested either in male or female, are and be and ought to be taken in the one as the other ...

Elizabeth legitimate, although she was recognised as Mary's heir in the event of her dying childless.

5 Mary Tudor, 1553-58

KEY ISSUES Was Mary I's allegiance to Catholicism and the Habsburgs as unrealistic as has been claimed by many historians? How successful was Mary in overcoming the problems she faced? Are attempts to portray Mary and the achievements of her reign in a more favourable light justified?

a) Background

Mary, the daughter of Catherine of Aragon, was 37 years of age when she came to the throne. During Edward VI's reign she had resisted Protestant reform just as strongly as she had under her father. While Somerset was in power she had been allowed to follow her Catholic religion in private, and she had remained on good terms with the Protector and Edward. With the swing towards Calvinism under Northumberland, increasing pressure had been put on Mary to abandon Catholicism and to conform to the doctrines of the Church of England. During this difficult period she had received constant support and advice from her Habsburg cousin, Emperor Charles V. It was fear of the Habsburgs that had prevented the reformers taking extreme measures against her. Mary was a proud woman, who resented the pressures put on her and was embittered by the treatment of her mother. This made her mistrust her English councillors when she became Queen, and lean heavily on advice from the imperial ambassador, Simon Renard.

When Mary proclaimed herself Queen on 11 July 1553, even Renard and Charles V had thought it a futile gesture. Yet when she entered London at the end of the month she was greeted with enormous enthusiasm. Political prisoners such as the Duke of Norfolk and Stephen Gardiner were released. Following the advice of Charles V, she showed leniency towards her opponents. Only Northumberland and two of his closest confederates were executed. Although some members of Northumberland's Council, like Cecil, were imprisoned, others, such as Paget, were allowed to join the new Privy Council. As a devout Catholic, Mary was insistent that England should return to the Church of Rome. At the same time, she was convinced that national safety depended on a close alliance with the Habsburgs. Her policy rested on the achievement of these two aims. Until 1555 this strategy appeared to be prospering, but thereafter Mary's popularity steadily declined until her death in 1558.

b) Assessments of Mary's Character

The cause for this unpopularity has generally been attributed to Mary's own character. Simon Renard's assessment that she was 'good, easily influenced, inexpert in worldly matters and a novice all round' was scarcely a flattering tribute. Elizabethan propagandists were eager to depict Mary as a weak and unsuccessful pro-Spanish monarch in order to highlight the achievements of their own queen. Protestant reformers reviled her as a cruel tyrant trying to enforce Catholicism through torture and burnings. This has produced a popular picture of 'Bloody Mary' – a stubborn, arrogant, Catholic bigot, who burned Protestants and lost Calais to the French because of her infatuation for Philip of Spain. In a modified form, this has been the view of many historians, but recently there have been attempts revise this critical appraisal. It has been pointed out that she showed skill and resolution in defeating Northumberland's attempted *coup d'état*. Mary has been criticised for indecision in the negotiations over the restoration of Catholicism to England and her marriage to Philip of Spain. This, it has been suggested, was in fact masterly political inactivity and pretended weakness, designed to win greater concessions from the Papacy and the Habsburgs, similar tactics to those that her sister Elizabeth used so successfully. Indeed, it is suggested that Mary had the broad support of the majority of the people until 1555. The problem was, it is suggested, not the weakness of Mary's character and policies, but her failure to produce an heir to consolidate her position. This, the outbreak of war with France and the declining economic position, was the real cause of Mary's growing unpopularity. On the basis of the existing evidence it is difficult to assess Mary's true character, and the present consensus of opinion lies somewhere between the two extremes.

c) System of Government

The system of central and local government remained fundamentally unchanged during Mary's reign. The Privy Council continued to be the centre of the administration. One of the main criticisms of Mary's Privy Council has been that it was too large to conduct business effectively. Certainly at times the membership did reach 43. In addition it has been claimed that the Council contained too many members who had no real political ability and who lacked administrative experience. The reason for this was that in the first few weeks of her reign Mary was forced to choose councillors from her own household, and from among leading Catholic noblemen who had supported her. By October several moderate members of Northumberland's Council had been sworn in as councillors, although they were never fully in the Queen's confidence. However, they supplied a nucleus of political ability and administrative experience previously lacking. Apart from this making the Council too large, it has been suggested that it caused strong rivalry between the Catholics, led by the Chancellor, Gardiner, and the moderates, led by Paget. However, it is now thought that, although there was disagreement, these two very able politicians co-operated closely to restore effective government. In any case, affairs of state were soon largely handled by an 'inner council' consisting of those experienced councillors who had reformed the Privy Council under Northumberland. Much of the original criticism of the Privy Council came from Renard, who was jealous of the Queen's English advisers and wished to maintain his own influence with Mary. The main problem was that Mary did not appear to exert any leadership, or show any real confidence in her Council. Frequently she did not consult the Privy Council until she had already decided matters of policy in consultation with Renard.

Previously it has been maintained that Parliament was strongly opposed to Mary's policies. This view has been modified by recent research. There seems to be little evidence that Mary controlled the House of Commons by packing it with Catholic supporters through rigged elections, and she had strong support from the higher clergy in the House of Lords, especially after the imprisonment and execution of Cranmer, Ridley and Latimer. Apart from the dislike of the Spanish marriage, both Houses seem to have co-operated with the administration throughout Mary's reign. As was the case in the Privy Council, there were lively debates and criticism of policy, but these were generally constructive. Like previous Parliaments, the main interest of the members centred on local affairs and the protection of property rights.

d) The Marriage Issue

Mary's political inexperience and stubbornness is shown in the first major issue of the reign – the royal marriage. The Privy Council was divided on the matter. There were two realistic candidates for Mary's hand. One was Edward Courtenay, Earl of Devon, who was favoured by Gardiner. The other was Philip of Spain, who was supported by Paget. Courtenay was a descendant of the Plantagenet kings and such a marriage would have strengthened the Tudor dynasty, but Mary favoured a closer link with the Habsburgs through Philip. It was not until 27 October that Mary raised the matter in Council, and then only to announce that she was going to marry Philip. This disconcerted Gardiner, who was blamed by Mary for the petition from the House of Commons in November, asking her to marry within the realm. Mary disregarded all opposition to her plans. On 7 December a marriage treaty, drafted by Mary, Paget, Gardiner and Renard, was presented to the Council. It was ratified at the beginning of January 1554. Mary had achieved her objective of forming a closer alliance with the Habsburgs. The terms of the treaty were very favourable to

England. Philip was to have no regal power in England, no foreign appointments were to be made to the Privy Council, and England was not to be involved in, or pay towards the cost of any of Philip's wars. If the marriage was childless, the succession was to pass to Elizabeth. In spite of these safeguards Mary's popularity began to ebb, as many people still thought that England would be drawn into Philip's wars and become a mere province of the Habsburg Empire.

e) Wyatt's Rebellion, 1554

By the end of January 1554, anti-Spanish feelings led to rebellion. Unlike the uprisings in 1549 this was a political conspiracy among the elites, and there was little popular support. The rebellion was led by Sir James Croft, Sir Peter Carew and Sir Thomas Wyatt. These men had all held important offices at Court under both Henry VIII and Edward VI. Although they had supported Mary's accession, they feared that the growing Spanish influence would endanger their own careers. The conspirators planned to marry Elizabeth to Edward Courtenay, whom Mary had rejected. Simultaneous rebellions in the West Country, the Midlands and Kent, were to be supported by the French fleet blockading the English Channel. The plan failed because the inept Courtenay disclosed the scheme to his patron, Gardiner, before the conspirators were ready to act. In any case, Carew, Croft and the Duke of Suffolk bungled the uprisings in the West Country and the Midlands. Wyatt succeeded in raising an army in Kent, and this caused real fear in the government because the rebels were so close to the capital. The situation was made worse because the troops sent under the Duke of Norfolk to Kent deserted to the rebels. Realising the danger, the Privy Council quickly raised forces to protect London. By delaying his advance too long, Wyatt allowed the government time to organise its troops and the rebels were trapped and defeated at Ludgate. The administration had had a bad scare, and Paget suggested leniency for the rebels for fear of provoking further revolts. Apart from Wyatt and the Duke of Suffolk, only Jane Grey and Guildford Dudley were executed. After a short imprisonment Elizabeth and Courtenay were released, and Elizabeth remained next in line to the throne. Even so, anti-Spanish feelings remained high. Philip's proposed coronation was postponed, and he only remained in England for a few months before returning to Spain.

f) The Restoration of Catholicism

Once the rebellion was defeated, the restoration of Catholicism (see page 94) became a political issue. Gardiner had lost Mary's favour over the Spanish marriage. In an attempt to regain it he pressed for the introduction of religious reform. He was opposed in the Council by Paget, who feared that such a policy would cause further unrest. Paget raised the matter in Parliament to try to block Gardiner's proposals. This introduced a very significant constitutional issue. Mary thought that religion was still part of the royal prerogative (see page 91). However, she was forced to concede that doctrinal changes could only be made through Parliament. In fact there was only minor opposition in the House of Commons to the restoration of Catholicism, and this was mainly caused by fears over property rights. Such worries were removed by guarantees that there would be no attempt to take back monastic and chantry lands already sold by the Crown. By 1555 all Henrician and Edwardian religious legislation had been repealed. There was comparatively little opposition to the actual religious changes. However, many historians consider that the policy of Mary and Archbishop Pole of persecuting and burning heretics began to turn even moderate opinion against her.

g) Financial and Economic Problems

i) Fiscal Reforms

The Marian administration was still faced by the financial problems that Northumberland had been trying to solve. To make matters worse, Mary had given away more crown lands in order to re-establish some monastic foundations. Consequently, it was important both to find new sources of government revenue and to increase the income from existing ones. To achieve this the Privy Council largely adopted the proposals put forward by the commissions in 1552. In 1554 drastic changes were made to the revenue courts. The Exchequer was restored as the main financial department. It took over the work of the Court of First Fruits and Tenths, which had dealt with clerical taxation, and the Court of Augmentations, which had administered income from monastic and chantry lands. The Court of Wards, which collected feudal taxation, and the Duchy of Lancaster, administering lands belonging to the monarch as Duke of Lancaster, retained their independence. It was planned to remove the large number of debased coins in circulation and to restore the full silver content of the coinage, but Mary's death meant that the scheme was not put into effect until 1560. The 1552 proposal to revise the custom rates, which had remained unchanged since 1507, was implemented. In 1558 a new Book of Rates was issued, which increased custom revenue from £29,000 to £85,000 a year. In 1555 a full survey of all crown lands was carried out. As a result rents and entry fines, a payment made by new tenants before they could take over the property, were raised in 1557. Mary died before these measures had any real effect, and it was Elizabeth I who benefited from the increased revenue brought about by these reforms.

ii) The Economy

During Mary's reign the general economic situation grew even worse, with a series of very bad harvests and epidemics of sweating sickness, bubonic plague and influenza. Towns were particularly badly hit, with high mortality rates and severe food shortages. The government's reaction was to continue the policy, started under Henry VIII, of restricting the movement of textile and other industries from the towns to the countryside. This, it was hoped, would prevent an increase in urban unemployment and reduce the number of vagrants seeking work. This, however, was short-sighted because what was really needed was an increase in the amount and variety of industries in both town and country, which would provide jobs for the growing number of unemployed. To achieve this the government needed to encourage the search for new overseas markets to replace the trade lost with the decline of the Antwerp market. In 1551 English ships had begun to trade along the north African coast, and between 1553 and 1554 Sir Hugh Willoughby was trying to find a north-east passage to the Far East (see page 68). However, until after 1558 successive English governments were too anxious to avoid offending Spain and Portugal to encourage overseas enterprise. It was not until the reign of Elizabeth I that any real progress was made in this direction.

h) Reform of the Army and Navy

In spite of the assurance that England would not be involved in Spain's wars, Mary's strong emotional attachment to Philip made it likely that England would be drawn into the continental conflict. As early as 1555 the Privy Council was reviewing the condition of the navy, which had been allowed to decline after Northumberland had made peace with France. A new building programme was started, improvements were made to the dockyards, and naval expenditure was increased through a new system of financing. Equal attention was paid to the army, especially after the outbreak of war in 1557. Arrangements for raising and maintaining the county militias were revised in the Militia and Arms Acts, which also improved the procedures for supplying arms and equipment. These reforms brought long-term improvements to England's military organisation.

j) Assessment of Mary's Reign

Philip II's visit to England early in 1557, and his success in drawing the country into his war against France, marked the final stage in Mary's growing unpopularity. The last two years of her reign saw rising anti-Spanish feelings, mounting opposition to religious persecution, and discontent with the adverse economic conditions. The war with France and the loss of Calais, England's last continental possession, united the knowledge and ideas to the examiner. To gain maximum credit you must demonstrate your ability to answer a question clearly, succinctly and relevantly. It is also essential that the examiner is able to understand what you are writing, so that good handwriting, grammar, punctuation and spelling are highly important.

An essay should consist of three parts: the introduction, the main body where the answer is developed, and a conclusion.

In the introduction you should demonstrate that you understand what the question is about, challenge any misleading assumptions contained in the question and indicate what approach you are going to adopt in answering it.

The main body of the essay is where you develop and analyse your factual evidence to demonstrate your grasp of the topic. Before you start writing you should underline the key words in the question and make sure that your answer is always focused on them. Each paragraph should be concentrated on a single major issue or topic and the points relating to which you wish to develop. Do not wander off the point. Irrelevance is penalised. Pargraphs should not be a series of separate statements, but should flow naturally from one point to the next to show the clarity of your thinking.

An essay answer should never just stop, it must reach a conclusion. The conclusion is where you draw together your arguments and sum up the answer to tie up any loose ends. However, avoid introducing any totally new material at this stage because it will just be confusing. Make sure that the examiner knows what your answer to the question is, and that you have rounded off your arguments. Remember this is the final impression you are leaving with the examiner. A poor conclusion can lose you marks, while a good conclusion might gain you marks for an otherwise average answer.

In the case of structured questions, you are likely to find that the wording used indicates clearly what you should do. However, much of the advice given above is still very relevant if you hope to score high marks.

Practise your writing skills by attempting one or other of these questions.

1. To what extent was Northumberland more successful in solving the mid-Tudor political problems than Somerset?

2a) What were the major political problems facing successive Tudor governments between 1547 and 1558? *(12 marks)*

b) Was Northumberland more successful than his predecessor Somerset in solving these problems? *(18 marks)*

Source-based questions on Chapter 2

With source-based material it is essential that you read the extract through several times until you are sure that you know what is being said and that you understand the meaning of all the words. Then you need to analyse the material to identify and note down the main points that are being made. You should also make sure that you are quite clear about when and in what context the extract was written, so that you have a firm background against which to form judgements about the material. Practise these skills with the following questions, remembering that you must make enough valid points to earn the marks allocated to each question.

1. The Succession
Read the extracts from the Letters Patent of 21 June 1553 on page 43, the Act Declaring Mary Legitimate (1553) on page 45 and the Act concerning Regal Power (1554) on page 45. Answer the following questions:

a) Who are **i)** 'our said late father' and **ii)** 'Lady Frances' in the first extract, and **iii)** 'the said Queen your mother' in the second extract? *(3 marks)*

b) Why are the words 'that female monarchs could not reign in England' in the third extract placed inside brackets? *(1 mark)*

c) What two arguments are used in the first extract against Mary and Elizabeth being allowed to succeed to the throne? *(4 marks)*

d) Which of these arguments is destroyed in the second extract? How is this done? *(2 marks)*

e) Why was it thought necessary to pass the Act of which the third extract is a part? *(4 marks)*

f) How valid is it to describe the Letters Patent of 21 June 1553 as revealing 'naked ambition without even a cloak of logical consistency to mask it'? (As always when answering questions with complicated wording, your first task is to identify the key words and phrases. What are the two key phrases in the quotation included in the question? A second task is to make sure that in your answer you explain the meaning of the key words/phrases.) *(6 marks)* and the advance of the Ottoman Turks along the river Danube. In the west, Philip II of Spain was to become increasingly concerned about stamping out heresy in his territories and checking the growth of Ottoman seapower in the Mediterranean. In the 1560s France was to be plunged into religious civil war. The struggle between the forces of the Reformation and the Counter Reformation would soon over-shadow the dynastic wars of the first half of the century. In economic terms the centre of power was moving away from the Mediterranean towards the Atlantic and north-western Europe. The loss of Calais in 1558 can be seen to have effectively ended English hopes of regaining her continental empire. After 1558 English foreign policy began to turn away from continental Europe towards the Atlantic and the colo-nial empires. A new policy was developing, for which control of the sea was of paramount importance. However, in 1547 England was still engaged in a bitter struggle with her neighbours, Scotland and France.

2 Henry VIII's Diplomatic Legacy

KEY ISSUES What was the basis of Henry VIII's foreign policy after 1542? To what extent was it over-ambitious? What problems did it leave his immediate successors?

England's foreign policy in the mid-sixteenth century, and especially during the reign of Edward VI, was greatly influenced by Henry VIII's diplomacy. Until recently many historians considered that Henry VIII had adopted the principle of holding the balance of power in western Europe. It was thought that in order to achieve this he allied with the weaker nations against the stronger to prevent any one country from becoming too powerful. Modern historians are sceptical about this theory. It is now believed that Henry allied with whichever side was most likely to win – and so help his dynastic ambitions. Henry's foreign policy seems to have been based on three main objectives: to regain the throne of France and outshine his great rival Francis I; to protect English cloth exports to the Netherlands by remaining on good terms with the Holy Roman Empire; and to gain greater control over Scotland, possibly by uniting the two countries. Until the 1530s, when the English Reformation had soured relations with the Catholic Empire, the most useful ally in attempting to achieve these aims had been the Emperor Charles V.

By 1542, mutual fears over France had restored good relations between England and the Empire. In particular, Henry VIII had seen the Franco-Scottish alliance, created by the marriage of James V and Mary of Guise in 1538, as a major threat to English security. Moreover, he appears to have been becoming increasingly concerned over the succession. Historians are divided about Henry's intentions at this stage. It is felt by some that his main aim was to unite Britain by the

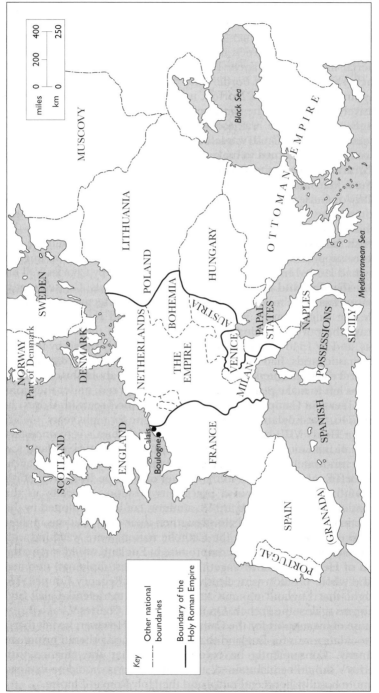

Europe c. 1550.

cavalry. After this victory Somerset was able to occupy all the main border strongholds. This gave England control of the border, but the success was not as decisive as it appeared because the English army was not strong enough to occupy the rest of Scotland. In any case, Somerset was anxious about domestic affairs in England, and left Scotland with his main army on 18 September.

b) Failure of the Anglo-Scottish Marriage Scheme

Defeat united the quarrelsome Scottish nobles, and they supported Mary of Guise in her opposition to England. While Somerset was in London, the Scottish Council met at Stirling and decided to ask the French for more help. It was suggested that, in return for French military aid, Mary Queen of Scots should marry Henry II's eldest son Francis. Meanwhile, England continued to negotiate with France. However, it soon became obvious that war would break out and that France was going to intervene in Scotland. English and French privateers attacked shipping in the English Channel and the North Sea, and the French began to build up their forces around Boulogne. In January 1548 Somerset issued an appeal to the Scots, called the *Epistle of Exhortation*, proposing a union between the two countries:

1 Who hath read the histories of time past doth mark and note the great battles fought betwict England and Scotland, the incursions, raids and spoils which hath been done on both parties … and shall perceive … that of all nations in the world that nation only beside England speaketh
5 the same language, and as you and we be annexed and joined in one island, so no people so like in manner, form, language, and all conditions as we are; shall not he think it a thing very unmeet, unnatural, and unchristian that there should be between us so mortal war, who in respect of all other nations be, and should be, like us two bretheren of
10 one island of Great Britain? … We offer equality and amity, we overcome in war and offer peace, we win [strong]holds and offer no conquest, we get in your land and offer England. What can be more offered and more proffered than the intercourse of merchandise, intercourse of marriages, the abolishing of all such our laws as prohibiteth
15 the same or might be impediment to the mutual amity … We intend not to disinherit your Queen but to make her heirs inheritors also to England. What greater honour can you seek unto your Queen than the marriage offered? What more meet marriage than this with the King's Highness of England?

For religious and political reasons the Scots preferred the French option. In June a French fleet landed an army of 10,000 troops in Scotland, and by August Mary Queen of Scots had been taken to France to be educated. Henry II proclaimed that France and Scotland were one country.

c) Stalemate in the Anglo-Scottish War

Meanwhile Somerset remained in London preoccupied with domestic issues. Although Carlisle, Berwick and Haddington Castle, the main English base north of the border (see the map below), were strengthened, Somerset seemed unwilling to take any decisive action. Lord Wharton, the Warden of the West March at Carlisle, and Lord Grey, Warden of the East March at Berwick, continued to hold the border with an army of 10,000 troops. However, without instructions from London, neither of them were prepared to take any initiatives. This encouraged the French troops in Scotland, reinforced with 8,000 Scots, to besiege Haddington, which had a garrison of 5,000 men. This placed Somerset in a dilemma. He was unwilling to leave London, and was worried by the French build-up of forces around Boulogne. Finally, judging correctly that Henry II would not attack Boulogne for fear of drawing Charles V into the war, he sent the Earl of Shrewsbury north with 12,000 infantry and 1,800 cavalry to relieve Haddington. Shrewsbury succeeded in forcing the besiegers to retreat, but Somerset soon ordered him to withdraw because of the high cost of maintaining his army. The siege was resumed, but after unsuccessfully assaulting the castle in October, the French began to tire of the expense of the war. In any case the Scottish nobles had begun to resent the French presence in Scotland, and Franco-Scottish relations deteriorated.

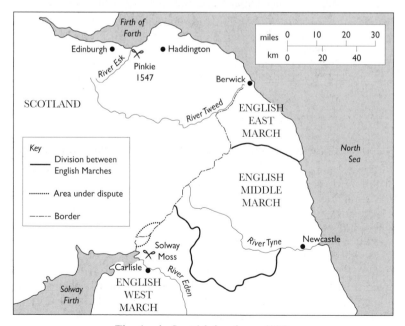

The Anglo-Scottish border c. 1550.

In January 1549 Somerset decided that Lord Wharton and Lord Grey were failing to take advantage of this situation. They were replaced by Lord Dacre and the Earl of Rutland, while the Earl of Shrewsbury was made Lord President of the Council in the North. However, before these changes had had time to take effect, affairs in the north were overshadowed by the peasant uprisings in England. Here again Somerset showed indecision. He was unwilling to withdraw troops from the border garrisons, and this delay allowed the situation in England to get out of control. Finally in August he was forced to withdraw troops from the north, and to recall the fleet to guard the English Channel against possible French attack. This caused the English to abandon Haddington and the other strongholds north of the border. Fortunately for England the French had already decided that the war in Scotland was too costly, and had redeployed their forces on the siege of Boulogne. Without support the Scots were too weak to launch any major attack on the north of England.

d) Assessment of Somerset's Leadership Qualities

Opinion among historians in their judgement of Somerset as a diplomat and a military commander is divided. It is widely agreed that although he was a good field general, as a Commander-in-Chief he was indecisive and afraid to delegate authority. He is seen as having failed to take advantage of his victory at the Battle of Pinkie, and showed little initiative in pressing home his dominant position along the border. Equally, it is agreed that it was Somerset's military indecision and his unwillingness to redeploy his troops in 1549 that allowed the popular uprisings to get out of hand; not, as it was once maintained, his humanitarian love of the common people. However, some historians consider that Somerset was not altogether to blame for the failure of his foreign policy. It is suggested that he had inherited an almost impossible diplomatic and military position in 1547. He was bound by Henry VIII's Will to arrange a marriage between Edward VI and Mary Queen of Scots in order to safeguard the English succession. In view of the hostility created by Henry VIII's earlier campaigns against the Scots, it is considered to be inevitable that Somerset would have been forced into war with Scotland to achieve this objective. It is also suggested that, given the Franco-Scottish alliance, England's weak military position in France, and the chronic shortage of money, this was a war which could not be won.

4 The Lord President Northumberland, 1550-53

> **KEY ISSUES** Was the ending of the war with France and Scotland almost inevitable? Why did diplomatic relations with both Charles V and Scotland deteriorate? What had made it necessary to find new trading areas? How successful were English attempts to achieve this? Northumberland has been condemned for weak leadership and for making a humiliating peace with France. Is such criticism justified?

By the autumn of 1549 foreign and domestic affairs had reached a critical point. The increasing Protestantism of the Church of England had alienated Charles V, and had left England in a very exposed position without a powerful continental ally. Attempts to enforce the agreed marriage between Mary Queen of Scots and Edward VI had not only failed, but had pushed Scotland into a marriage alliance with France. England was committed to a ruinously expensive war on two fronts, the cost of which was adding to the already serious problems at home. Henry II was not slow to take advantage of this situation. He declared war in August and took personal command of the siege of Boulogne. Somerset's failure to deal with all these problems led to his fall, and gave Northumberland the opportunity to seize power.

a) Peace Negotiations with France

The war had become increasingly unpopular with both the elites and the general public. High levels of taxation were undermining the economy and provoking rising hostility towards the government. For some time the Privy Council, especially Lord Paget, had been advocating peace as a means of restoring financial and economic stability (see page 41). Although Northumberland was much more sympathetic to these views than Somerset had been, during the winter of 1549 he was fully occupied in gaining control of the government. The French took advantage of this power vacuum to built up their forces around Boulogne. They were able to break English lines of communication between Boulogne and Calais, which threatened to isolate the garrison of Boulogne under the command of Lord Huntingdon. However, an English fleet decisively defeated a strong force of French galleys in a battle off the Channel Islands. This gave England control of the Channel, and meant that Boulogne could be supplied by sea. However, as the government was virtually bankrupt, Northumberland was unable to raise an army to lift the siege. Attempts to persuade Charles V to extend the treaty protecting Calais to Boulogne failed. Even so, Henry II was afraid that Charles V would intervene to help England. Northumberland was keen to end the war so that he could consolidate his own position.

In January 1550 a delegation led by Lord Russell was sent to France to negotiate peace. They proposed that in return for ceding Boulogne the French should pay a full ransom, and re-open negotiations about a marriage between Mary Queen of Scots and Edward VI. Henry II took full advantage of England's weak position and refused to make any concessions. Finally, Northumberland, strongly supported by Paget, persuaded the Privy Council that they had no alternative but to accept the French terms. The Treaty of Boulogne was signed on 28 March 1550. Under the terms of the Treaty the English had to withdraw from Boulogne in return for a ransom of 400,000 crowns. At the same time they had to remove their remaining garrisons from Scotland, and agree not to renew the war unless provoked by the Scots. Finally, there was to be a perpetual defensive alliance between England and France. Boulogne was handed over to the French on 25 April, and the English garrison was sent to reinforce Calais.

Although the Treaty of Boulogne removed the danger of French invasion and ended the crippling expense of the war, the potential crisis still remained. The humiliating peace and alliance with a traditional enemy was seen as a national disgrace, and added to Northumberland's unpopularity. In spite of this, he negotiated with the French for a marriage between Edward VI and Henry II's daughter Elizabeth. It was agreed that Elizabeth would come to England when she was twelve years of age, and would have a dowry of 200,000 crowns. The alliance was ratified in December 1550 in return for English neutrality in continental wars. England's international position was still very weak, and was made worse because lack of money forced Northumberland to run down both the army and the navy. The Habsburgs remained hostile, particularly as the Church of England was beginning to swing towards more extreme Calvinist doctrines (see Chapter 4). In many respects England had returned to the position of weakness and isolation which had resulted from the failure of Henry VIII's foreign policy in 1528. Certainly the Treaty of Boulogne marked the end of the phase of policy initiated by Henry VIII, during which the reconquest of French territories was a major goal.

b) Relations with the Holy Roman Empire

England's relations with the Holy Roman Empire deteriorated steadily. Apart from disliking the Anglo-French alliance, Charles V was particularly annoyed by the attempts of the English reformers to force Princess Mary to abandon her Catholic faith. A consequence of this cooling of relations was a breakdown in commercial contacts with the Netherlands, which had been protected by the *Intercursus Magnus* since 1496. In April 1550 Charles issued an edict allowing the Catholic Inquisition to arrest any heretics in the Netherlands. This outraged many English merchants. Although the edict was modified to exclude foreigners, it helped to bring about the collapse of the Antwerp cloth market, as many Flemish clothworkers fled to England to avoid persecution. The situation was further complicated by disputes over piracy in the English Channel. It was not until December 1550 that Charles made any attempt to restore good trading relations, and then only from fear that England would be driven into a closer alliance with France.

c) Anglo-Scottish Relations

Anglo-Scottish relationships were in an equally poor state. When Northumberland withdrew the remaining English garrisons from Scotland he left the French in total control. However, the Scottish nobles and the Protestant Lowlanders were becoming increasingly hostile towards the French, fearing that Scotland would become a mere province of France. The fall of Somerset had left a confused situation on the English side of the border. Lord Dacre and the Earl of Rutland at Carlisle and Berwick had no clear policy to follow. In 1550 Northumberland decided to take personal control of affairs along the border by making himself General Warden of the North, with Lord Wharton as his deputy. To end the constant minor disputes which threatened the uneasy peace, Sir Robert Bowen was ordered to survey the border. He reported that an area fifteen miles by four miles was under dispute. After strengthening Berwick and Carlisle, Northumberland returned to London, leaving Lord Dacre to negotiate a settlement of the line of the border with the Scottish wardens. Progress was very slow, and it was not until a French fleet landed supplies and troops in Scotland in February 1551 that negotiations began in earnest. Finally, in March 1552, it was agreed that the border was to be restored to the line held before Henry VIII's Scottish campaigns.

d) Worsening Relations with the Continent Powers

During 1551 Northumberland maintained his policy of neutrality towards the continental powers. Charles V continued to disapprove of the increasing Protestantism of the Church of England, and considered that English foreign policy was unpredictable. It was not until March 1552, when war broke out again between Charles V and Henry II, that Anglo-Imperial relations began to improve. Northumberland resisted French pressure to join in the war against the Holy Roman Empire, and Charles V was more conciliatory over English trade with the Netherlands. Finally, by June 1552, good diplomatic relations were restored between the two countries. Then, when the French invaded Lorraine and the Netherlands, Charles V reminded England that she was bound under treaty obligations to assist the Empire if the Netherlands were attacked. The garrison at Calais was reinforced, but

England still took no active part in the war. Even so, England's relations with France deteriorated. The second half of the ransom for Boulogne remained unpaid and French privateers had begun to attack English shipping. Although England was in no position to take any military action, the French feared an Anglo-Imperial alliance and were careful to avoid open confrontation. In January Northumberland, proposed to act as mediator between France and the Empire. This action was prompted by fears over Edward VI's declining health and the illness of Charles V. The French were not interested in making peace, and in June 1553 the negotiations collapsed.

e) The Beginning of New Policies Aimed at World Trade

The decline of the Antwerp cloth market and the breakdown in commercial relations with the Empire prompted English merchants to urge the government to find new markets. In 1547 the Italian explorer, Sebastian Cabot, had been given a pension of £100 a year to live in England and help to discover new lands. In 1551 William Hawkins opened up trade in cloth, timber, saltpetre, iron and sugar along the Barbary coast. By 1553 English ships were trading as far as the Gold Coast in West Africa. However, this was the full extent of the trading effort because, although English merchants were eager to break into the trade with the Far East, their ships and their navigation were too poor to attempt the sea routes around the Cape of Good Hope. In any case, until after 1558, successive English governments did not encourage Atlantic exploration for fear of offending Spain and endangering the Anglo-Habsburg alliance. To overcome these difficulties the cartographer and geographer, John Dee, proposed finding a north-east passage to the East. In 1552 a joint-stock company was established with Sebastian Cabot as its governor, to which city merchants and members of the Privy Council each contributed £25. In May 1553 Sir Hugh Willoughby was put in command of three ships, and given sailing orders drawn up by Sebastian Cabot. The Privy Council gave Willoughby letters of introduction to the ruler of China. Willoughby and two of the ships were lost in Lapland in 1554. His second-in-command, Richard Chancellor, succeeded in reaching the port of Archangel in the White Sea and established diplomatic links with Ivan IV, the Tsar of Muscovy. In 1553 the Muscovy Company was founded to establish trade between the two countries (see page 152). This early English exploration, and improvements to the dockyards and the navy begun in 1555, were to come to fruition later during the reign of Elizabeth I.

At the time these events were overshadowed by the death of Edward VI in 1553 and the ensuing constitutional crisis. Obviously the question of the succession in England was of great interest to both Charles V and Henry II. The accession of the Catholic Mary Tudor, with her strong attachment to the Habsburgs, would probably bring England into the war on the imperial side. Charles V was strongly in favour of this solution, which would enhance his war effort and restore Catholicism in England. From the French point of view this would have been a far from ideal situation. Consequently, they favoured a succession that would leave Northumberland in power, and possibly produce a situation where they could intervene in favour of the claims of Mary Queen of Scots. Although the imperial diplomats were convinced that Mary Tudor's claim to the throne would be ignored, Northumberland's plans to replace her with Lady Jane Grey failed because of lack of support among the English aristocracy and gentry (see page 45).

f) Assessment of Northumberland's Leadership Qualities

Historians have revised their opinion of Northumberland as a diplomat. In the past he has been seen in the same light as by his contemporaries; as a man who betrayed the national honour by giving Boulogne back to France and then adopted a policy of cowardly appeasement. Recently historians have begun to see him not only as a good soldier, but also as a quite capable diplomat. They consider that, faced as he was by an impossible military situation and a bankrupt Exchequer, he was taking the only sensible course by making peace. With Mary Queen of Scots safely in France, it is felt that there would have been little point in prolonging hostilities with Scotland. Furthermore, Northumberland is seen as taking decisive action by assuming personal control as Lord Warden to investigate the petty disputes along the Scottish border. He is also seen to have possessed the ability to delegate authority, by leaving Lord Dacre, with his wide experience of northern affairs, to reach a final settlement. It is suggested that the ceding of Boulogne was equally pragmatic. Historians now consider that, even with the support of the Habsburgs, England would not have been able to hold Boulogne – a town which, apart from being a symbol of national prestige, was of no real value to the country.

5 Mary Tudor, 1555-58

> **KEY ISSUES** Why, despite its apparent advantages, was was Mary's marriage alliance with Spain and the Habsburgs unpopular? How and with what consequences was England drawn into war with France? The loss of Calais may not have been a national disaster, but why is Mary still blamed for the failure of her foreign policy?

As expected, Mary's successful bid for the throne once again placed England securely in alliance with the Holy Roman Empire. Her proposed marriage with Philip of Spain, Charles V's eldest son, meant that England would be firmly allied with the most powerful country in western Europe. Moreover, as the Netherlands were to form part of Philip's inheritance, England's main commercial outlet would be secure. However, in spite of these apparent advantages, many Englishmen feared that the alliance would lead to a renewal of the war with France.

a) French Plots to Prevent an Anglo-Spanish Alliance

There were similar fears in France, and the French ambassador, Noailles, worked hard to promote opposition to the marriage. He was certainly involved in the conspiracy to marry Courtenay to Princess Elizabeth and place them both on the throne (see page 49). That the government was well aware of these problems and their implications is clear from a report in November 1553 to Charles V from Simon Renard about a conversation between Mary, Lord Paget and Renard concerning the English succession. The rival claimants would be the Queen of Scotland, the affianced bride of the Dauphin, who had a real right by descent; the Lady Frances, wife of the Duke of Suffolk, who would also have a claim if the Queen of Scotland were excluded as having been born abroad, as being a Scotswoman and married to the Dauphin of France; and the Lady Elizabeth:

1 who claimed the crown because of the disposition of the late King
   Henry, authorised by an act of Parliament that had never been repealed
   ... As for the Lady Elizabeth, the Queen would scruple to allow her to
   succeed because of her heretical opinions, illegitimacy, and characteris-
5 tics in which she resembled her mother; and as her mother had caused
   great trouble in the kingdom, the Queen feared that Elizabeth might do
   the same, and particularly that she would imitate her mother in being a
   French partisan ... But [if Mary died childless] it seemed to him [Paget]
   that, as Parliament had accepted the Lady Elizabeth as proper to
10 succeed, it would be difficult to deprive her of the right she claimed
   without causing trouble.

The failure of the plot, and the defeat of Wyatt in Kent, ended French hopes of preventing the Anglo-Spanish alliance. Although the marriage agreement appeared to safeguard England against being involved in Philip's wars, there was a clause which stipulated that Philip should aid Mary in governing her kingdom. This provided a loophole which Philip could use to draw England into the continental conflict.

b) War with France

By July 1555 it had become apparent that Mary was not going to bear any children and that her health was deteriorating, so ending Philip II's hopes of an heir to rule in England. In October, still plagued by ill-health, Charles V abdicated his titles and went into retirement at the age of 55. His brother Ferdinand succeeded to his German lands, while Philip became King of Spain and ruler of the Netherlands, Naples, Sicily, Milan and the New World. Philip left England to assume his new responsibilities. However, Stephen Gardiner, the most trusted of Mary's English councillors, died in November 1555, and she was anxious for Philip to return to England to advise her. He paid little attention to her pleas until March 1556, when the war with France broke out again. Philip came to England to enlist support, but the Privy Council was totally opposed to any involvement in the war. England was still in a weak military position in spite of reforms to the army and navy (see page 51). Then, however, fresh French plots against Mary came to light, and the Privy Council reluctantly declared war on France.

In July 1556 the Earl of Pembroke was sent to France with an army of 7,000 men. There they joined the army commanded by Philibert, Duke of Savoy, who won a decisive victory over the French at St Quentin in 1557. At the same time the English fleet attacked the French coast. These combined operations forced the Duke of Guise, commanding the main French army, to return to France from Italy. In retaliation for the English intervention he launched an attack on Calais. Unfortunately the government had already been forced to borrow heavily to equip the army and navy sent to the continent, and were unable to afford to send reinforcements to Calais. The defences of Calais had been neglected, and Lord Wentworth, the Commander, was unable to make any real resistance. Calais fell on 13 January 1558, and the French soon occupied the remainder of the English strongholds around the port.

In response to this humiliating defeat the government raised an army of 7,000 troops, supported by a fleet of 140 ships, to invade France. The intention was not to recapture Calais, but to attack Brest. Finding Brest too heavily defended the English force captured the smaller port of Le Conquet. Meanwhile Henry II and Philip II were camped near Amiens with armies of 45,000 men. Instead of the expected decisive battle, the two monarchs decided to negotiate. At first Philip demanded the return of Calais to England as part of the settlement. Then Mary died in November 1558, and Philip abandoned his former ally. Under the terms of the Peace of Cateau-Cambresis in April 1559 France and Spain signed a lasting peace treaty. Philip married Henry II's daughter Elizabeth, and the French guaranteed not to intervene in Philip's Italian territories. France retained Calais, the last English possession on the continent.

c) Assessment of Mary's Leadership Qualities

Although historians no longer agree with the opinion of Mary's contemporaries that the loss of Calais was a national disaster, they continue to condemn her conduct of foreign affairs. It is still considered that Mary's stubbornness, and her almost total reliance on her Spanish advisers, made England's military debacle between 1557 and 1558 almost inevitable. There is some sympathy for Mary over the way in which Philip II blatantly used England for his own ends, but it is felt that she was too infatuated with Philip and the Habsburgs to take reasonable precautions to protect English interests. It is thought that in 1553 the Habsburgs had serious intentions of turning England into a permanent base, to complete the 'Habsburg ring' encircling France. Philip's unpopularity in England, and the realisation in 1555 that Mary was incapable of producing an heir, is seen as the reason for abandoning this strategy. This, it is thought, is what convinced Philip in 1556 to use English troops for short-term military gains, and for his desertion of his ally after the death of Mary in 1558.

Working on Chapter 3

You will have noticed that that the difficulties and weakness of England's diplomatic position between 1547 and 1558 followed much the same pattern as the political problems at home. Section 1 gives you a brief background to the diplomatic situation in the mid-sixteenth centure, and your notes should be organised so as to provide answers to the questions posed in the issues box. Follow the same procedure for each of the remaining sections and this will give you all the basic points you need in order to understand mid-Tudor foreign policy. Be sure to note the extent to which religion was becoming a major factor in Western European diplomacy. You should then decide what were the major changes taking place in English foreign policy. Finally, refer back to your notes on Chapter 2 to help you to come to some conclusions about how effective Somerset, Northumberland and Mary Tudor were in conducting foreign affairs.

Answering structured and essay questions on Chapter 3

This section looks at the way to answer the 'success' type of question.

1a) What were the major diplomatic problems facing successive Tudor governments between 1547 and 1558? *(12 marks)*
  b) How successful was Somerset in carrying out the foreign policy that he inherited from Henry VIII? *(18 marks)*
2a) Outline the major changes in English policy towards France and the Habsburg empire between 1547 and 1558? *(12 marks)*
  b) Was Mary Tudor's foreign policy as unsuccessful as it was once considered? *(18 marks)*

Question 1a) requires you simply to dicuss the major changes in English foreign policy, while for 1b) you will be expected to analyse the evidence and make your own judgements on Somerset's diplomatic and military capabilities. Question 2a) is only asking you

Summary Diagram
Foreign Policy, 1547-58

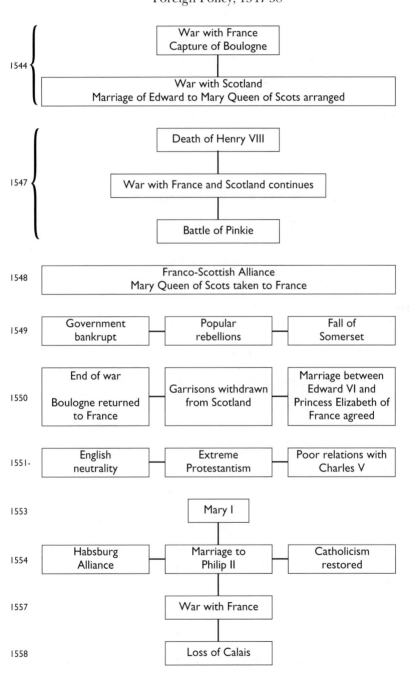

1544
- War with France
- Capture of Boulogne

War with Scotland
Marriage of Edward to Mary Queen of Scots arranged

1547
- Death of Henry VIII
- War with France and Scotland continues
- Battle of Pinkie

1548
Franco-Scottish Alliance
Mary Queen of Scots taken to France

1549
Government bankrupt — Popular rebellions — Fall of Somerset

1550
End of war

Boulogne returned to France — Garrisons withdrawn from Scotland — Marriage between Edward VI and Princess Elizabeth of France agreed

1551-
English neutrality — Extreme Protestantism — Poor relations with Charles V

1553
Mary I

1554
Habsburg Alliance — Marriage to Philip II — Catholicism restored

1557
War with France

1558
Loss of Calais

to write about relations with France and the Habsburgs, so do not discuss English policy with Scotland unless it has a direct bearing upon the other two countries. For the second part of the question you have to know why Mary Tudor's foreign policy used to be condemned, how and why opinions have changed, and then use your own judgement to decide the extent to which it was successful or unsuccessful.

Essay questions of this type are similar, but remember that you need to read them carefully to pick out the key words which tell you what sort of answer the examiners are expecting.

1. Why was Somerset unsuccessful in carrying out the foreign policy that he inherited from Henry VIII?
2. Was Northumberland's foreign policy any more successful than that of his predecessor?
3. With what success did Mary Tudor try to change the direction of English foreign policy?

In question 1 the key words are 'Why was', 'unsuccessful', 'foreign policy' and 'inherited from Henry VIII'. Notice that this question contains the assumption that Somerset was unsuccessful. You need to discuss this assumption, indicating how far you agree with it. You also need to identify what was Henry VIII's foreign policy, and to reach conclusions about how Somerset tried to implement it and whether he was successful or unsuccessful. If you judge him to have been unsuccessful, you have to decide whether his failure was the result of the impracticability of the policies, or of his own shortcomings as a leader.

The key words in question 2 are, 'Was ... foreign policy any more successful' and 'his predecessor'. To answer the question you need to a) analyse Northumberland's foreign policy, b) consider the problems he faced and c) decide whether his solutions were more effective than those of Somerset.

The key words in the third question are, 'With what success ... change the direction of English foreign policy'. For this question you need to analyse how and why Mary Tudor changed English foreign policy, and then to decide whether she was successful or unsuccessful.

Source-based questions on Chapter 3

Quite frequently when answering source-based questions you are asked to decide about the reliability of the evidence as in question 2d) below. This type of question is asking you not only to make judgements about the evidence itself, but also about the person(s) who wrote it. This means that you have know the context in which the extract was written. You should ask yourelf the following questions – were the author(s) likely to be accurate or biased, was the document written from first hand knowledge or from hearsay, for what purpose was the document written and for whom? In the case of question 2d) Simon Renard is writing a report to Charles V so what are the implications as to its accuracy?

1. Relations with Scotland

Read the extract from Somerset's Epistle of Exhortation to the Scots (January 1548), given on pages 62. Answer the following questions:

a) What is meant by 'intercourse of merchandise' (line 13)? *(1 mark)*
b) Explain the significance of the offer of 'intercourse of marriages' (line 14). *(3 marks)*
c) Explain in detail Somerset's assertion that 'no people [are] so like in manner, form, language, and all conditions as we are'. *(8 marks)*
d) What proposal was Somerset making to the Scots? *(3 marks)*
e) What were the consequences of the Scottish decision not to accept the English proposal? *(5 marks)*

2. Renard on the English Succession, 1553

Read the extract from Renard's report to Charles V, given on page 70, and answer the following questions:

a) What is meant by 'scruple' (line 3)? *(1 mark)*
b) What three reasons does Renard give as the basis of a possible rejection of the claim of Mary Queen of Scots to the succession? *(3 marks)*
c) What evidence might Renard have presented to suggest that Paget's prediction was sound? *(4 marks)*
d) What was Renard's purpose in writing his report? What are the implications of this for its likely accuracy? *(6 marks)*
e) Why was the English succession of interest to Charles V? Support your answer with evidence from outside the extract. *(6 marks)*

4 Religious Change, 1547–58

POINTS TO CONSIDER

This chapter discusses the main religious changes (the changes themselves and their effects) during the reigns of Edward and Mary. A major debating point is, 'Were most people still Catholic during this period or did they just conform to the religion of the monarch?'. You need to estimate how successful the reformers were in introducing Protestant doctrines into the Church of England during the reign of Edward VI. You then need to consider whether Mary would have succeeded in permanently returning England to the Church of Rome if she had lived long enough.

KEY DATES

1536		The Ten Articles introduced some Lutheran doctrines
1539		The Great Bible in English circulated to parishes
1539		The Six Articles restored full Catholic doctrine
1547		Repeal of the Six Articles
1548		Act for the dissolution of chantries
1549	Jan	Act of Uniformity and the Book of Common Prayer
	Jun	Introduction of the First Prayer Book
1552		Act of Uniformity. Second Book of Common Prayer – introduced some Calvinistic doctrines
1553		Catholic mass re-introduced
1554	Nov	Cardinal Pole came to England as papal legate and England was formally reconciled with the Church of Rome
	Dec	Re-introduction of the heresy laws
1555	Oct	Bishops Ridley and Latimer burnt at the stake
1556	Mar	Archbishop Cranmer burnt at the stake
1558		Deaths of Mary and Pole
1559	May	Act of Supremacy restored Henrican anti-papal laws

1 Introduction

> **KEY ISSUES** How have historians' views about mid-Tudor religious attitudes changed? To what extent had religion become an important issue in English politics? Why and how had religion become an issue in foreign affairs, and what problems did this cause successive governments between 1547 and 1558?

a) Changing Views of Mid-Tudor Religious Attitudes

Views among historians about the significance of religion in mid-

Tudor England have changed during recent years. It is now felt that there was a much greater degree of religious compromise in England than on the continent, and that as a result religion itself was not a cause of crisis. However, religion is seen as having a considerable influence on the political, social and economic changes which were taking place at the time. Consequently, religion can be seen as contributing directly, or indirectly, to potential crises, such as in the Western Rebellion of 1549, or in the attempt by Northumberland to stop Mary Tudor succeeding to the throne in 1553.

In the past, historians saw the Edwardian Reformation as a period of remarkable toleration during which reformed religion became firmly established in the country. They considered it to have been followed by five years of Catholic repression and persecution, which failed to stamp out English Protestantism. Such views are no longer widely held. It is increasingly doubted whether Protestantism had taken much of a hold in England by 1553. Indeed, it is now suggested that Catholicism had wide popular support among the lower orders in both the towns and the countryside. At the same time, it is now thought that there was much less animosity between English Catholics and Protestants than was previously believed. It is true that there were extremists on both sides, just as there were individuals prepared to die for their faith. However, the vast majority of people are seen as being very moderate in their outlook, and as being prepared to accept whatever doctrine was held by the ruling regime. It is this that is seen as being the basis for religious compromise in England. The whole of the period between 1547 and 1553 is held to be one of marked toleration. Even the Marian religious repression is regarded as very mild in comparison with the persecution on the continent.

b) Religion as a Political Issue

At the same time religion had become a political issue. There is wide agreement that Henry VIII's motives in breaking away from Rome were much more political than religious. The English Reformation put the Church firmly under the control of the State. It also removed England from the authority of the Pope; a source of outside interference which was highly resented among the English elites. Ecclesiastical wealth replenished the Exchequer, which had been almost bankrupted by Henry VIII's unsuccessful wars of the 1520s. On the surface, the Crown was the main beneficiary of the English Reformation. Yet, once religion had come to the forefront of the political arena, it created problems for the monarchy. Religious differences deepened the rift between political factions at Court. Henry VIII had to tread a cautious path between the conservative Catholic and reforming Protestant parties. However, by 1547 he had decided that the safest way to protect the succession and the royal supremacy was to give control of the Privy Council to Somerset and the reformers.

During the renewed power struggle which followed the fall of Somerset in 1549 some of the leading Catholic conservatives were able briefly to regain their positions in the Privy Council. However, once Northumberland had consolidated his position, they were expelled. Northumberland's attempt to change the succession in 1553 was prompted not only by personal ambition, but also by the desire to prevent the Catholics regaining power under Mary Tudor. Even so there was still a great deal of toleration. A majority of the ruling elites favoured moderate reform, but Catholic politicians were not excluded from government purely for religious reasons. Stephen Gardiner, the leading Catholic bishop, spent most of Edward VI's reign in prison, but this was largely because he refused to co-operate in any way with the Privy Council. When Mary Tudor came to power in 1553 there was no great purge of Protestant politicians. Indeed, men like Paget were given high office. It is true that Mary did not trust such men, but neither did she have great confidence in her English Catholic councillors. Given that among the elites moderate reformers were in a majority, the fact that Mary came to the throne at all is a sign of the toleration in England. She was supported as the legitimate heir in spite of her religion. During her reign most politicians and civil servants were prepared to conform to her religious views. It was not her religion, but the ending of the royal supremacy and her marriage to Philip II of Spain that provoked most opposition.

c) Religion as an Issue in West European Diplomacy

Religious differences made politics and diplomacy much more complicated. Religion had become an important diplomatic issue in foreign affairs in western Europe. This meant that English foreign and domestic policy had to avoid antagonising the major continental powers. For this reason the question of the English succession became a matter of international interest. It was partly fear over the succession and the threat of Catholic intervention that prompted Henry VIII to go to war with Scotland and France in 1542 and 1544. He failed to achieve his aim of uniting England and Scotland through the marriage of Prince Edward and Mary Queen of Scots. Somerset tried to force the Scots into agreeing to the marriage by continuing the war. The failure of this plan led to bankruptcy in 1549, and forced Northumberland into making peace and maintaining a policy of weak neutrality. Moreover, the Catholic powers on the continent were able to use Mary Queen of Scots, because she was a legitimate Catholic claimant to the English throne, as an excuse to intervene in English affairs, particularly under Elizabeth I.

Religion was the cause of other difficulties for English relationships with the continent. England's main ally and trading partner was Charles V. However, Charles was a leading supporter of the Counter Reformation. He was therefore opposed to religious reform in

England, fearing that it would lead to a swing towards Protestantism. Consequently, the English Reformation had brought the country to the brink of war with the Holy Roman Empire. Somerset is seen by many historians as being careful to introduce only moderate religious reforms in order to avoid offending Charles V. When Northumberland began to allow the Church of England to become more Calvinist, Charles withdrew his support, so leaving the country in a very weak military and diplomatic position with no major continental ally. During the reign of Mary I England was drawn into a Catholic-Habsburg alliance, which eventually led to war with France and the loss of Calais. However, this must be seen more as a dynastic alliance, with religion playing a secondary role.

2 The Henrician Church in 1547

> **KEY ISSUES** Although the Church of England had broken away from the Church of Rome, to what extent was it still essentially Catholic in 1547? What success had the reformers had in introducing Protestant doctrines into England by the time of Henry VIII's death?

In order to see the significance of the religious changes which took place between 1547 and 1558 it is necessary to understand the doctrinal position in the Church of England at the death of Henry VIII. From the time Henry had made himself Head of the English Church in 1534 he had been under pressure to formulate an acceptable doctrine. The reform party led by Cranmer had advocated the introduction of moderate Lutheran ideas. On the other hand, the pro-Catholic, conservative faction led by Gardiner had favoured a policy of minimum change to the basic Catholic doctrines. During the period 1534 to 1546 royal favour swung between the two groups. The first major statement of doctrine, the Act of the Ten Articles, came in 1536. This Act was passed when the reformers were in the ascendancy, and introduced a number of Lutheran doctrines into the Church of England. Three years later the conservatives regained royal favour and the Act of the Six Articles was passed to remove many of the Lutheran beliefs. Such shifts of policy meant that by 1547 the doctrines of the Church of England were a compromise and contained many inconsistencies which were unacceptable to reformers and conservatives alike.

a) Catholic Doctrines in the Church of England

When Henry VIII died the main articles of faith in the Church of England were in line with traditional Catholic orthodoxy. The Eucharist was clearly defined in the Catholic form of transubstantiation – the sacramental bread and wine being transformed at consecration

into the body and blood of Christ. The Lutheran form of consubstantiation – the belief that the sacramental bread and wine remained
unchanged at communion, but that there was a real presence of Christ
in the heart of a true believer – was no longer accepted in the Church
of England. Only the clergy were permitted to take communion in both
the bread and the wine, while the laity were again restricted to taking
only the sacramental bread. The Catholic rites of confirmation,
marriage, holy orders and extreme unction had been re-introduced,
alongside the previously recognised sacraments of the Eucharist,
penance and baptism. The laity were still required to make regular
confession of sins to a priest, and to seek absolution and penance.
English clergy were no longer allowed to marry, and those who had
married before 1540 had had to send away their wives and families, or
lose their livings. Although there was no specific statement on the existence of Purgatory, the need for the laity to do 'good works' for their
salvation had been reinstated. The singing of masses for the souls of the
dead was held to be 'agreeable also to God's Law'. It was for this reason
that the chantries, where a priest sang masses for the souls of the
founder and his family, were not closed down at the same time as the
monasteries. Paintings and statues of the saints were still allowed in the
churches, although the laity were instructed not to worship them. Many
of the processions and rituals of the Catholic Church were still prac-
tised, because it was maintained that they created a good religious
frame of mind in those who witnessed them.

b) Protestant Doctrines in the Church of England

Although the Church of England remained fundamentally Catholic
in doctrine, it had adopted a number of Protestant practices by 1547.
Services were still conducted in Latin, but Cranmer's prayers and responses of the Litany in English had been authorised in 1545. Greater
importance was attached to the sermon, and the Lord's Prayer, the
Creed and the Ten Commandments had to be taught in English by
parents to their children and servants. Similarly the Great Bible of
1539 was the authorised English translation which replaced the Latin
Vulgate Bible. Moreover, the elite laity were allowed to read the Great
Bible in their own homes, unlike on the continent where often only
the Catholic clergy were allowed to read and interpret the Bible. The
practice of the Church of England with regard to some Catholic
doctrines was ambiguous. Saints could be 'reverenced for their excel-
lent virtue' and could be offered prayers, but the laity were forbidden
to make pilgrimages to the shrines of saints or to offer them gifts,
because it was maintained that grace, salvation and remission of sins
came only from God. At the same time, the number of Holy Days –
days on which, like Sundays, the laity were expected to attend church
and not to work – had been reduced to 25. Finally, in sharp contrast
to Catholic countries, there had been no monasteries in England

since 1539, when even the larger monasteries had been closed by royal order, and their possessions had been transferred to the Crown.

Attempts between 1534 and 1546 to establish a uniform set of articles of faith for the Church of England had only succeeded in producing a patchwork of doctrines that often conflicted. Until 1547 this ramshackle structure was held together by the Henrician treason and heresy laws. Anyone breaking, or even questioning, the statutes and proclamations defining the doctrines of the Church of England was liable to confiscation of property, fines, imprisonment, or execution. Similarly the censorship laws prevented the printing, publishing, or importation of books and pamphlets expressing views contrary to the doctrines of the Church of England.

3 The Edwardian Church, 1547-49

> **KEY ISSUES** Why was the new regime so cautious about introducing religious reform? Is it true to say that the continued lack of any clear doctrinal policy had placed the Church of England in a weak position by 1549? Were the Western Rebellion and other uprisings in 1549 an indication of popular support for Catholicism, or a protest against increasing pressures on the traditional way of life of the lower orders?

The accession of Edward VI, who had been educated as a Protestant, roused the hopes of English reformers that there would be a swing towards more Lutheran, and possibly Calvinist, doctrines. Somerset's appointment as Lord Protector in 1547 established the reform party firmly in power, as intended under the terms of Henry VIII's Will. Somerset was a moderate Protestant, but although he was devout, he had no real interest in theology. He was religiously tolerant, and favoured a cautious approach towards reform. Although he is reputed to have had Calvinistic leanings, and, certainly, exchanged letters with John Calvin, there is little evidence of such influences when he was in power. The reformers were in the majority in the Privy Council. However, among the bishops, while nine led by Cranmer and Ridley supported reform, ten led by Gardiner and Edmund Bonner, Bishop of London, opposed change. The remaining eight bishops were undecided on doctrinal issues. But all the bishops fully supported the royal supremacy and the separation from Rome. With such an even balance of opinion among the bishops, the Privy Council moved very cautiously on matters of religious reform.

a) Attitudes Towards Reform

The attitude towards reform outside the immediate government circle is difficult to assess. A majority of the elites seems to have been

approved. However, there was still no really clear statement on the existence, or otherwise, of Purgatory. Any form of the worship of saints, although not banned, was to be discouraged, while the removal of statues, paintings and other images was encouraged. However, Cranmer's Book of Common Prayer was a mixture of Lutheran and Catholic beliefs. Fast days were still to be enforced and no change was to be made in the number of Holy Days. The new communion service followed the order of the old Latin mass, and the officiating clergy were expected to continue to wear the traditional robes and vestments. Most importantly, no change was made to the doctrine of the Eucharist, which was still defined in the Catholic terms of transubstantiation. This was a fundamental point that angered many of the more radical reformers, who continued to urge the government to adopt a more Protestant definition of the sacrament of communion.

The Privy Council hoped that these cautious measures would satisfy the majority of moderate reformers, without outraging the Catholic conservatives. Although any clergy who refused to use the new service were to be liable to fines and imprisonment, no penalties were to be imposed on the laity for non-attendance. This can be interpreted as a hope by the Privy Council that they could coerce the more recalcitrant minority among the parish clergy, while not antagonising the undecided majority among the laity. The government decided to continue with its policy of educating the laity in Protestant ideas which it had introduced in July 1547. Bishops were instructed to carry out visitations to encourage the adoption of the new services, and to test whether parishioners could recite the Lord's Prayer and the Ten Commandments in English. The effectiveness of either the legislation, or the education programme, depended on whether the bishops and elites would enforce them. There was opposition in Cornwall, Devon, Dorset and Yorkshire. However, most of the country seems to have followed the lead of the aristocracy and gentry in accepting moderate Protestantism.

e) Popular Reaction – the Western Rebellion, 1549

It is difficult to judge to what extent underlying opposition to these changes in religion contributed to the fall of Somerset in 1549. Certainly only the Western Rebellion was directly linked with religion, and even there underlying economic and social discontent played an important part in causing the uprising. To a certain extent the rebels in the west were complaining about enclosures and about the gentry, whom they accused of making use of the Reformation to seize church land for their own enrichment. Such views were held in other areas during the popular uprisings of 1549 (see pages 38 and 124), but only in the West Country was direct opposition to the new Act of Uniformity the central issue.

The popular discontent began in Cornwall in 1547, when the local archdeacon, William Body, who was disliked both for his Protestant views and for his personal greed, began to try to introduce religious reforms. He was mobbed by a hostile crowd at Penryn and fled to London. In April 1548 he returned to Cornwall to supervise the destruction of Catholic images in churches. At Helston Body was set upon, and killed, by a mob led by a local priest. As the troublemakers dispersed quickly the authorities made only a few arrests. But they hanged the ten ringleaders. Then in 1549 the Cornish lower orders, fearing that the Act of Uniformity was going to be imposed on them, rose in rebellion and set up an armed camp at Bodmin. Because of the hostility expressed by the rebels towards landlords, only six of the more Catholic local gentry joined the uprising. However, the West Country elites were very unwilling to take any action against the rebellion on behalf of the government. The main leaders of the rebels were local clergy, and it was they who began to draw up a series of articles listing demands to stop changes in religion. In Devon there was an independent uprising at Sampford Courtenay. By 20 June the Devon and Cornish rebels had joined forces at Crediton, and three days later they set up an armed camp at Clyst St Mary. Local negotiations broke down, and the rebels began to blockade the nearby town of Exeter with an army of 6,000 men. Lord Russell, who had been sent to crush the rebellion, was hampered by a shortage of troops and a lack of local gentry support. As a result it was not until August that the rebels were finally defeated.

Some of the demands put forward in the final set of articles drawn up by the rebels clearly illustrate their religious conservatism and other grievances felt in the West Country:

1   I. First we will have the general counsel and holy decrees of our fore-fathers observed, kept and performed, and who so ever shall speak against them, we hold them as heretics.
    II. Item we will have the Lawes of our Sovereign Lord Kyng Henry the
5   VIII concerning the Six Articles, to be used as they were in his time.
    III. Item we will have the mass in Latin, as was before, and celebrated by the priest without any man or woman communicating with him.
    IV. Item we will have the Sacrament hung over the high altar, and there to be worshipped as it used to be, and they whiche will not therto
10   consent, we will have them die like heretics against the holy Catholic faith.
    VII. Item we will have holy bread and holy water made every Sunday ... Images to be set up again in every church, and all other ancient olde Ceremonies used as heretofore, by our mother the holy
15   Church.
    VIII. Item we will not receive the newe service because it is but lyke a Christmas game ...
    X. Item we will have the whole Bible and all books of scripture in English to be called in again ...

20 XIV. Item we will that the halfe parte of the abbey lands and Chantry lands, in every mans possession, howsoever he came by them, be given again to two places, where two of the chief Abbeys used to be in every County ...

The government clearly saw these articles as ultra-conservative demands for a return to Catholicism, and they were vigorously repudiated by Cranmer and the leading theologians among the reformers. It was claimed that the rank and file had been misled by, as Somerset put it, 'seditious priests, to seek restitution of the old bloody laws' for their own purposes. It was the manner in which the articles were phrased, just as much as their content, that offended the government. Unlike the usual wording of petitions to the Crown by rebels, such as the 'We pray your grace' used by Robert Kett in the same year, each of the Western rebels' articles began 'Item we will'. Such lack of deference and respect, along with denials of the royal supremacy in the articles themselves, was seen as a greater threat to the stability of society and the State than the rebellion itself.

Cranmer was particularly enraged by such insubordination, and by the suggestion in article XIII that no gentleman should have more than one servant. It was this that enabled the government to accuse the rebels of being dangerous social anarchists, and so distract attention from their attack on religious change. In any case the government theologians found no difficulty in pouring scorn on the lack of doctrinal knowledge in the articles. Their demands for the return of images and the old ceremonies were dismissed as idolatrous, and the old mass was described as being more like games held during the Christmas season. Even greater scorn was poured on the suggestion in article VIII that they rejected the new services in English because as Cornishmen it was a language that they did not understand. Historians agree that the rebels showed little knowledge of either Protestant or Catholic doctrines, but suggest that such ignorance in the West Country probably reflected similar confusion among the great mass of the population. Whether this is true or not, these demands do show that, in the West Country at least, many of the laity were still strongly attached to the familiar traditions of the old Church.

4 The Edwardian Church, 1550-53

KEY ISSUES Why did religious reform become increasingly radical under Northumberland? In what ways did the English Church become more Protestant? After six years of reform was the Church of England firmly Protestant by 1553?

a) Doctrinal Power Struggle

When Northumberland gained power in 1550 religious reform became more radical. It is difficult to decide whether this suggests that the government considered that there was no widespread opposition to religious change, or that they thought the recent suppression of the popular uprisings was sufficient to prevent any further unrest. Possibly, as is thought by many historians, the changes came about because of political in-fighting in the Privy Council. What is certain is that by 1553 the Church of England had become Protestant.

In view of his reconversion to Catholicism before his execution in 1553, many historians do not think it likely that Northumberland was a genuine religious reformer. Other historians feel that his support for such a Protestant enthusiast as John Hooper against Cranmer and Nicholas Ridley, Bishop of London, in the doctrinal dispute during the autumn of 1550 (see page 90) does show that he was interested in religious reform. This is a question which, without fresh evidence, is unlikely to be resolved. Certainly the first moves towards introducing more radical Protestantism seem to have arisen from the political expediencies following Somerset's fall from power. After the arrest of Somerset in October 1549 it appeared that the conservative faction supported by Northumberland might seize power. They planned, with the help of Charles V, to make Princess Mary regent for the young Edward VI. However, neither Charles V nor Mary supported the scheme which, in any case, would not have been practical in view of Edward VI's increasing support for Protestantism. Meanwhile, Northumberland, having used the conservatives to strengthen his position on the Privy Council, then switched his allegiance to the more radical Protestant reformers. This political struggle within the Privy Council continued when Parliament met in November. Attempts by conservatives to repeal the 1549 Act of Uniformity and strengthen the power of the bishops were defeated. In December Parliament approved measures to speed up the removal of popish images and old service books from the churches, and set up a commission to revise the procedures for the ordination of priests.

By February 1550 Northumberland was firmly in control of the Privy Council, and the conservatives were driven out of office (see page 40). To strengthen his position still further and to prevent a possible conservative backlash, Northumberland moved against the more conservative of the bishops. Gardiner, the most able of the pro-Catholics, was already imprisoned in the Tower of London. In July he was ordered by the Privy Council to agree to the doctrines of the Church of England. He refused, and was sentenced to stricter terms of confinement. Bishop Bonner of London, already imprisoned by Somerset, was retried and deprived of his diocese. He was replaced by Ridley, then Bishop of Rochester, who was an enthusiastic reformer. During the next year active reformers were appointed as bishops of

Rochester, Chichester, Norwich, Exeter and Durham. These changes cleared the way for more sweeping religious reforms. The Catholic laity and clergy, deprived of their main spiritual leaders, offered little opposition, although some pro-Catholic pamphlets were circulated.

b) A Swing Towards More Extreme Protestantism

The first move to introduce more radical Protestantism was initiated by Ridley in London, where he ordered all altars to be removed and replaced by communion tables in line with the teachings of the Calvinists and other reformed Churches. In other dioceses the destruction of altars proceeded unevenly, and depended on the attitudes of the local elites and clergy. At the same time the Parliamentary Commission's proposals to change the form of the ordination of priests were introduced, and instructions were issued to enforce the first Act of Uniformity. The new form of ordination, which was basically Lutheran, soon caused controversy. The major change – which empowered priests to administer the sacraments and preach the gospel instead of offering 'sacrifice and [the celebration of] mass both for the living and the dead' – satisfied moderate reformers. It removed the supposedly superstitious references to sacrifice, Purgatory and prayers for the souls of the dead. However, it did not please some of the more extreme reformers, especially because it made no attempt to remove any of the 16 ceremonial vestments, such as the mitre, cope, tippet, or stole, normally worn by bishops and priests while conducting services. These were regarded as superstitious by many of the reformed Churches, whose clergy wore plain surplices. John Hooper, who had been invited to become Bishop of Gloucester, complained that the form of ordination was still too Catholic and started a fierce dispute with Ridley over the question of vestments. As a result he refused the offered bishopric, and in July he began a campaign of preaching against the new proposals. At first it appeared that Northumberland was sympathetic and supported Hooper, but in October he was ordered to stop preaching, and in January 1551 he was imprisoned for failing to comply. Finally he was persuaded to compromise and was made Bishop of Gloucester, where he introduced a vigorous policy of education and reform. But he complained that both laity and clergy were slow to respond.

c) Measures to Make the Church of England Fully Protestant

During 1551 Northumberland consolidated his position. This cleared the way for a major overhaul of the Church of England. Cranmer was in the process of revising his Prayer Book, to remove the many ambiguities that had caused criticism. Further action was taken against the remaining conservative bishops. Gardiner was finally deprived of the diocese of Winchester in February, and in October reformers were appointed at Worcester and Chichester. These moves ensured that there would be a majority among the bishops to support the programme of religious changes that was being prepared.

i) Doctrinal Changes

Parliament was assembled in January 1552 and the government embarked upon a comprehensive programme of reform. In order to strengthen the power of the Church of England to enforce doctrinal uniformity, a new Treason Act was passed. This made it an offence to question the royal supremacy or any of the articles of faith of the English Church. At the same time, uncertainties over the number of Holy Days to be recognised was ended by officially limiting them to 25. In March the second Act of Uniformity was passed. Under the new Act it became an offence for both clergy and laity not to attend Church of England services, and offenders were to be fined and imprisoned. Cranmer's new Book of Common Prayer became the official basis for church services, and had to be used by both clergy and laity. The new prayer book was based upon the scriptures, and all traces of Catholicism and the mass had been removed. The Eucharist was clearly defined in terms of consubstantiation (see page 80), although there are some suggestions that Cranmer was moving towards a more Zwinglian or Calvinistic definition of the Eucharist as commemorative of Christ's sacrifice or the Last Supper. Extreme reformers did not approve of the new service because communicants were still expected to kneel, and they considered this to be idolatrous. Some historians attribute such objections to the Calvinism of Hooper and another extreme reformer, John Knox. It is also suggested that theirs was the influence behind the instructions sent to bishops to speed up the replacement of altars by communion tables, and to stop their clergy from wearing vestments when conducting services.

ii) Further Attacks on the Wealth of the Church

While these measures were being introduced, the government began a further attack on church wealth. In 1552 a survey of the temporal wealth of the bishops and all clergy with benefices worth more than £50 a year was undertaken. The resultant report estimated that these lands had a capital value of £1,087,000, and steps were taken to transfer some of this property to the Crown. The bishopric of Durham provides a typical example of this secularisation. Bishop Tunstall of Durham was arrested in October 1552 and imprisoned in the Tower of London. It was then proposed that his diocese should be divided into two parts. Durham itself was to be allocated £1,320 annually, and a new see of Newcastle was to be given an annual income of £665. This left an annual surplus of £2,000 from the income of the original bishopric, which was to be expropriated to the Crown. In the event, this proposal never came into effect because of the death of Edward VI. At the same time, commissioners had been sent out to draw up inventories and to begin the removal of all the gold and silver plate still held by parish churches, and to list any items illegally removed since 1547. The commissioners had only just begun their work of confiscation when the King died and the operation was brought to an end, but not before some churches had lost their medieval plate (see page 98).

Some historians have seen this further attack on church wealth as yet another example of the greed of Northumberland. Others maintain that it was necessary if the Church of England was to be thoroughly reformed. Recently these actions have been interpreted as an expedient to improve royal finances after the bankruptcy resulting from the wars against France and Scotland. To Marxist historians it was clear evidence of the growing commercialism of the aristocracy and gentry, who were pressurising the government for a further redistribution of ecclesiastical wealth. Yet another explanation is that it was a political move to strengthen the control of the Church by the State. Without fresh evidence and research it is difficult to decide which one, or whichever combination of these explanations, is nearer the truth.

d) Assessment of the Edwardian Church

What is certain is that the death of Edward VI and the fall of Northumberland brought this phase of the English Reformation to an abrupt end. The Forty-two Articles which had been drawn up to list the doctrines of the new Protestant Church of England never became law. It is generally agreed that by 1553 the Edwardian Reformation had resulted in a Church of England that was thoroughly Protestant. There is less unity over whether its doctrines were basically Lutheran, or to what extent they were influenced by Zwinglian, or Calvinist ideas. However, it is clear that, although the doctrines of the Church of England had been revolutionised, the political and administrative structure of the Church had remained unchanged. There is equal agreement that there is insufficient evidence at present to decide whether the people of England had wholeheartedly embraced the Protestant religion. Research at a local level has so far provided conflicting evidence. Although a majority of the landed elites and those in government circles seemed to favour moderate Protestantism, only a few of them did not find it possible to conform under Mary I. Many of the lower clergy and a majority of the population seem to have been largely indifferent to the religious debate. Only in London, the counties circling London and East Anglia does there appear to have been any widespread enthusiasm for the Protestant religion. Even there, a study of the county of Essex indicates more enthusiasm among the authorities in enforcing Protestantism than among the general public in accepting it. Earlier interpretations which indicated wild enthusiasm for either

Protestantism or Catholicism are now treated with caution. It is considered that Protestantism, if not widely opposed, received only lukewarm acceptance.

5 The Marian Church, 1555-58

> **KEY ISSUES** How and with what success did Mary restore first Catholicism and then Roman Catholicism to England? If the majority of the population were moderate Catholics or undecided, why did Mary's religious policies eventually make her so unpopular? Was it only a shortage of finance that stopped the Marian bishops fully restoring Roman Catholicism in England? Why is it difficult to decide what people really thought about religion by 1558?

a) The Religious Situation in 1553

While it is difficult to assess Northumberland's religious views, there is no doubt about those of Mary I. Some historians have described Mary as courageous, gentle and sympathetic. Others see her as being proud, arrogant, bigoted, narrow-minded and stupid. These views have not been greatly altered by recent research. However, it is agreed that she was passionately attached to the Roman Catholic religion. In 1553 no one in England doubted that Mary, after her 20 years of resistance to the royal supremacy for the sake of her religion, would restore Roman Catholicism. There is good evidence to suggest that it was just as much Edward VI's wish to preserve Protestantism, as Northumberland's personal ambition, that led to the attempt to exclude Mary from the throne. Mary and her Catholic supporters saw the failure of the scheme as a miracle, and she was determined to restore England to the authority of Rome as quickly as possible. What Mary failed to realise was that her initial popularity sprang, not from a desire for a return to the Roman Catholic Church, but from a dislike of Northumberland, and respect for the legitimate succession.

Her main supporters in England and abroad urged caution. Both Charles V and Pope Julius III warned her not to risk her throne by acting too rashly. Cardinal Reginald Pole, appointed as Papal Legate to restore England to the authority of Rome, stayed in the Netherlands for a year before coming to England. Whether this was because Charles V refused to allow the Cardinal to leave until the planned marriage between Philip and Mary had come to fruition, or whether it reflected Pole's natural caution about returning to his native land and a possibly hostile reception, is difficult to decide. Even Gardiner, Mary's most trusted English adviser, who had consistently resisted reform, was unenthusiastic about returning to papal authority. Mary singularly failed to realise the political implications of restoring Roman Catholicism to England. A return to papal authority would mean an end to the royal supremacy, which was strongly supported by the ruling and landed elites. Even the most ardent of the leading conservatives had been firm in their allegiance to the Crown and the Tudor State. It is agreed that the major causes of Mary's widespread unpopularity by the end of her reign, apart from the religious persecution, were the return to papal authority and the Spanish marriage. Most of the population regarded this as interference by foreigners and an affront to English nationalism.

b) The Restoration of Catholicism

However, in 1553 there was no doubt about Mary's popularity and the elites rallied to her support. The aristocracy and gentry were initially prepared to conform to Mary's religious views, and the bulk of the population followed their example. But some 800 strongly committed Protestant gentry, clergy and members of the middle orders left the country and spent the remainder of the reign on the continent. Such an escape was less easy for the lower orders, and most of the 274 Protestant activists executed during Mary's reign came from this group. At the beginning of the reign even the most zealous of the urban radicals were not prepared to go against the mainstream of public opinion, and waited to see what would happen. Certainly, when Mary, using the royal prerogative, suspended the second Act of Uniformity and restored the mass, there was no public outcry.

This lack of religious opposition was apparent when Parliament met in October 1553. Admittedly, the arrest and imprisonment of Cranmer, Hooper and Ridley, along with other leading Protestant bishops, removed the major source of opposition in the House of Lords. After a lively, but not hostile debate, the first step towards removing all traces of Protestantism from the Church of England was achieved with the passing of the first Statute of Repeal. This Act swept away all the religious legislation approved by Parliament during the reign of Edward VI, and the doctrine of the Church of England was restored to what it had been in 1547 under the Act of the Six Articles.

Although Mary had succeeded in re-establishing Catholicism, her advisers had managed to persuade her into some caution. There had been no attempt to question the royal supremacy, or to discuss the issue of the church lands which had been sold to the laity. Both these issues were likely to provoke a more heated debate.

Opposition to Mary's proposed marriage to Philip II of Spain and the consequent rebellion (see page 49) meant that further religious legislation was postponed until the spring of 1554. Gardiner, anxious to regain royal favour after his opposition to Mary's marriage (see page 49), tried to quicken the pace at which Protestantism was removed by persuading Parliament to pass a bill to re-introduce the heresy laws. He was successfully opposed by Paget, who feared that such a measure might provoke further disorder. Thwarted in this

> **The first Statute of Repeal, 1553**
> **[Having repealed the Edwardian religious legislation.]**
> 1 And be it further enacted by the authority aforesaid, that all such
>   divine service and administration of Sacraments as were most com-
>   monly used in the realm of England in the last year of the reign of our
>   late Sovereign Lord King Henry VIII shall be, from and after the
> 5 twentieth day of December in the present year of our Lord God
>   1553, used and frequented throughout the whole realm of England
>   and all other the Queen's majesty dominions; and that no other kind
>   nor order of divine service nor administration of sacraments be,
>   after the said twentieth day of December, used or ministered in any
> 10 other manner, form or degree within the said realm of England, or
>   other the Queen's dominions, that was most commonly used, minis-
>   tered and frequented in the said last year of the reign of the said late
>   King Henry VIII.

direction, Gardiner proceeded to turn his attention to Protestant clergy. The Bishops of Gloucester, Hereford, Lincoln, Rochester and the Archbishop of York were deprived of their sees, and were replaced by committed Catholics. In March 1554 the bishops were instructed to enforce all the religious legislation of the last year of Henry VIII's reign. Apart from ensuring a return to 'the old order of the Church, in the Latin tongue', these injunctions demanded that all married clergy should give up their wives and families, or lose their livings. The authorities largely complied with these instructions, and some 800 parish clergy were so deprived. Although some fled abroad, the majority were found employment elsewhere in the country.

c) Return to the Church of Rome

Cardinal Pole finally arrived in England in November 1554, and this marked the next decisive stage in the restoration of Roman Catholicism. Parliament met in the same month and passed the second Statute of Repeal. This Act ended the royal supremacy, and returned England to papal authority by repealing all the religious legislation of the reign of Henry VIII back to the time of the break with Rome. However, to achieve this Mary had to come to a com-promise with the landed elites. Careful provision was made in the Act to protect the property rights of all those who had bought secu-larised church land since 1536. This demonstrates that Mary had to recognise the authority of Parliament over matters of religion. It meant that she had to forgo her plans for a full-scale restoration of the monasteries. Instead she had to be content with merely returning the monastic lands, worth £60,000 a year, still held by the Crown.

Elizabethan Protestant Church of England. In 1555 the Westminster synod approved the establishment of seminaries in every diocese for the training of priests, but shortage of money limited the programme to a single creation at York. This meant that the majority of the parish clergy remained too uneducated, and lacking in evangelical zeal, for the new laws to have any immediate impact on the laity. Mary's death in November 1558 came too soon for Catholic reform to have had any lasting effect. That is not to say that if Mary had lived longer, Catholicism would not have gained wider support than the significant minority, who clung to their faith after the establishment of the Elizabethan Church.

e) Assessment of the Church of England in 1558

To assess the state of religion in England in 1558 is just as difficult as it is to measure the advance of Protestantism by 1553. It is almost impossible to decide to what extent the bulk of the population had any particular leanings towards either the Protestant or the Catholic faiths. While it is easy to trace the changing pattern of official doctrine in the Church of England through the acts and statutes passed in Parliament, it is a much greater problem to determine what the general public thought about religion. At present the consensus among historians is that the ruling elites accepted the principle of the royal supremacy, and were prepared to conform to whichever form of religion was favoured by the monarch. Although the lower orders are generally considered to have had a conservative affection for the traditional forms of worship, it is thought they were prepared to follow the lead of the local elites. Whether the religious legislation passed in Parliament was put into effect very much depended on the attitudes of the local elites, and to a lesser extent those of the parish authorities. For this reason detailed research into parish and county communities is being undertaken in the hope of revealing the religious attitudes among the laity. Such research uses the evidence of wills, parish registers, church wardens' accounts and court records to delve into local religious attitudes. Although such sources can be helpful, they are often difficult to use. The following extract from the churchwardens' accounts for the parish of Stanford in the Vale illustrate some of these problems.

1   **1552** Item. in expences at Abingdon [a neighbouring town] going before the kings Comissioners about our church's goods.
Item. paid for a book of common prayer in English in the time of schism.
1553 Item. in expences at Abingdon when the Church goods were
5   carried to King Edward's comissioners.
Item. to the mason for setting up the high altar.
1554 Item. to Henry Snodnam gent for a table with a frame which served in the church for the communion in the wicked time of schism.

Item. to Edythe Whayne for mending copes and vestments.
10 **1556** Item. in expences to Abingdon of my lord Cardinal Pole's visitation.
Item. in expences to Abingdon to buy images.
Item. for writing a bill to answer certain Articles of Religion proposed by my lord Cardinal Pole to certain of the clergy and the Justices of the
15 Peace to discuss.

These accounts show quite clearly that religious legislation was being enforced in the parish, but the problem is to decide what, if anything, this reveals about the attitudes of the local people. It might be assumed that, because the parish had complied with generally unpopular pieces of legislation for setting up communion tables and surrendering church plate, the parishioners were in favour of Protestantism. On the other hand, the speed with which the high altar was replaced in 1553 and the reference to Edward VI's reign as the wicked time of schism, might equally be interpreted as showing an attachment to Catholicism. In any case the record of religious changes might merely indicate that the local authorities were conforming to government policy, and show nothing about popular attitudes. This is very much the difficulty encountered in local studies. Lancashire elites are shown to have actively resisted the introduction of reformed religion, while in Essex Protestantism is seen to have been enthusiastically enforced. In neither case is much revealed about the views of the general public. Nor are historians confident that the findings for one county are typical for the local region, far less for the whole country. One recent study, based on Devon and Cornwall, does seem to have succeeded in finding out more about popular attitudes. This is an area where, because of the Western Rebellion, historians expected to find strong religious conservatism. However, the study, while revealing no zeal for Protestantism, uncovered equally little enthusiasm for Catholicism. Indeed, by 1558 passivity and indifference seem to have replaced religious fervour in the West Country.

In general it appears that by 1558 the majority of people in England were still undecided about religion. Among the elites there was strong support for the royal supremacy, but they were willing to follow the religion of the legitimate monarch. The mass of the population do not appear to have had strong formalised convictions, and in most cases they were prepared to follow the lead of their social superiors. Although there were small minorities of committed Protestants and Catholics, neither religion seems to have had a strong hold in England when Mary I died. When Elizabeth I came to the throne the country was willing to return to a form of moderate Protestantism. However, during her reign deeper religious divisions began to appear, and the unity of the Church of England ended.

You need to remember that religion was a major issue in mid-Tudor England, and that it interlocked with every other aspect of life. Religion is a controversial topic and the thinking about its role in mid-Tudor England is still changing. Therefore, it is important that your notes should not just help you to answer questions specifically on religion, but should also indicate where religion played an important part in politics, foreign policy, and social and economic change. Section 1 is designed to give a brief introduction to the way in which views about mid-Tudor religion are changing, and the way in which religion was decoming a political and diplomatic issue. Section 2

Summary Diagram
Religious Change, 1547-58

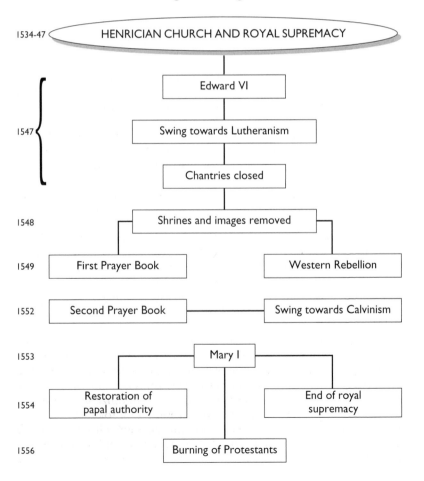

examines the state of the Church of England at the time of Henry VIII's death. It is important that your notes give you a clear picture of the Henrican Church in 1547 so that you can use it as a yardstick when assessing the religious changes between 1547 and 1558. The remaining sections examine in detail the religious changes that took place under Somerset, Northumberland and Mary Tudor, and assess the wider implications of these changes. You should structure your notes around the questions posed in the issues boxes. Make sure you have a sound grasp of how and why the the state of the Church of England had changed by 1549, 1553 and 1558.

Answering structured and essay questions on Chapter 4

This section looks at how to approach the 'results/consequences' type of question.

a) To what extent had the Church of England become more Protestant by 1549? *(20 marks)*
b) What were the main consequences of Somerset's religious reforms? *(20 marks)*

Notice that individual examination boards give different weightings to structured questions. In this case, parts a) and b) have the same weighting. Therefore, you need to spend roughly an equal amount of time on each part.

Question a) requires you to make a comparison between the the state of the Church of England in 1547 and in 1549, outlining the changes that had taken place, and then assessing to what degree the Church had become more Protestant.

Question b) asks you to assess the results of religous change by 1549. The results could, among other things, be: the closure of chantries, the fall of Somerset, doctrinal confusion, iconoclasm, freedom of religious debate and popular discontent and rebellion. What you need to do is to exercise your judgement in deciding which of these were the main consequences and provide the evidence to support your choice.

'What were the consequences of Mary Tudor's attempt to restore Roman Catholicism to England?'

Here again you are being asked to use your judgement in assessing the evidence. Clearly, a major consequence was the restoration of Roman Catholicism, and you will have to indicate how this was achieved. You have ask yourself whether the marriage to Philip of Spain and the alliance with the Habsburgs was an essential part of this process, and if so what were the consequences. The Wyatt Rebellion was a short-term consequence, but did it have any longer-term significance? The re-introduction itself had a whole series of both long- and short-term consequences . Did the persecution of heretics just make

Mary unpopular with certain sections of the population, or did it also ensure that the Church of England became permanently Protestant after 1558? What was the reaction of the general public – did most people really care about religion or did they just conform to the views of whoever was in power? If Mary had not died so young would England have remained permanently Roman Catholic?. These are some of the issues that you might discuss. Remember you have to supply the evidence to support whichever line of argument you choose to adopt.

Source-based questions on Chapter 4

Some source-based questions will ask (as in question 4d) below) you to 'use your own knowlege'. This means that you need to supply enough background points to earn the alloted marks. Usually 1 mark is given for each accurate piece of information, such as, in this case, that he was the Archbishop of Canterbury. Before attempting the exercises below, identify all the questions which are requiring you to use your own knowledge in order to answer them.

1. The First Edwardian Act of Uniformity, 1549
Read the extract from the First Edwardian Act of Uniformity, given on page 84, and answer the following questions:

a) Which previous Act was replaced by this legislation? *(1 mark)*
b) Who was the Archbishop of Canterbury, referred to in lines 1-2? *(1 mark)*
c) What were the implications of the words 'to the most sincere and pure Christian religion taught by the Scripture, as to usages of the primitive Church' (lines 4-6)? *(6 marks)*
d) Why was the government anxious to introduce a uniform order of worship? *(2 marks)*

2. The Articles of the Western Rebels, 1549
Read the extract from the articles of the Western Rebels, given on pages 87-88, and answer the following questions:

a) Were the rebels demanding a return to Catholicism or an extension of Protestantism? *(1 mark)*
b) What was the 'new service' referred to in line 16? *(1 mark)*
c) What were the implications of article X (lines 18-19)? *(5 marks)*
d) Which phrase in another article is making a similar demand to article X? *(1 mark)*
e) What was it about the form (as opposed to the content) of the articles that particularly antagonised the Privy Council? *(2 marks)*

3. The First Statute of Repeal, 1553
Read the extract from the first Statute of Repeal, given on page 95, and answer the following questions:

a) Why did Mary need an Act of Parliament in order to return the country to Catholic doctrine and forms of worship? *(3 marks)*

b) What was being reversed by the Act? *(2 marks)*

c) In what ways was the Act not a complete restoration of Catholicism? *(5 marks)*

4. *Religious change at a local level, 1552-56*

Study the extract from the churchwardens' accounts, given on page 98, and answer the following questions:

a) Which Act of Parliament required parishes to purchase an English prayer book? How long had it taken the churchwardens of Stanford to comply with the new law? What can be deduced from this? *(5 marks)*

b) What 'Church goods' are being referred to in line 5? Why were they being taken to the King's commissioners? *(4 marks)*

c) What can be deduced from the use of the phrase 'in the wicked time of schism' (line 8)? *(3 marks)*

d) Using your own knowledge, explain briefly the reference to 'my lord Cardinal Pole' in line 14 *(3 marks)*

5 A Crisis in Society?

POINTS TO CONSIDER

This chapter examines the ways in which the social structure changed between the late middle ages and the mid-sixteenth century. Your first task is to consider the advantages and disadvantages of using social models when studying the past. You then need to assess the extent to which the late medieval social structure had changed by 1522. You also need to decide who benefited from the redistribution of monastic lands, and what effect this had had on elite society by 1558. Finally, you should decide whether it was likely that mid-Tudor popular unrest was caused by social problems.

KEY DATES

1349>	The Black Death and further epidemics of bubonic plague drastically reduced the population
1390>	Serfdom among the lower orders coming to an end
1400 to 1500	Low population, low prices, low rents and high wages created a 'golden age' of lower order prosperity
1470>	Loss of political and economic power by the aristocracy and growth in royal authority
1500>	Increasing population growth and inflation forced up prices and rents and created unemployment.
1500>	Growing commercialisation helped to increase the influence of the gentry and yeomen
1530s	Growing shortage of land created competition among the elites
1539>	Closure of the monasteries enabled large-scale re-distribution of land among the elites
1540>	Rapid population growth caused rapid inflatioin and rising unemployment
1549	July Kett's Rebellion in Norfolk

1 Theories of Social Change

KEY ISSUES How do Marxist and Revisionist theories of social change differ? What, if any, effect did religion have on social change? Why are changes in population levels thought to quicken the pace of social chance? Why do such theories have to be used with caution? Why is it unlikely that the popular uprisings in 1549 were the result of social change?

The sixteenth century was a highly significant period because major changes were taking place within English society. However, because social change is such a slow, long-term process, it is virtually impossible to measure it over short periods of time such as the period between 1547 and 1558. Instead, historians have to try to assess what stage the series of complicated structural changes which had begun in the fourteenth century (see page 13) had reached by the middle of the sixteenth century. At the same time they have to consider what effects, if any, particular events, such as the Reformation, were having on society. Only then is it possible to reach any conclusions about whether there was a mid-century social crisis, or the extent to which social change contributed to any of the problems facing Tudor governments at that time.

It is widely agreed that by the middle of the sixteenth century, although the actual shape of the social structure had altered very little, the changes that were taking place were causing stresses within the fabric of society. However, the extent to which any such tensions contributed to the popular unrest in 1549 is not clear. This uncertainty reflects the lack of agreement about the nature of the changes taking place. During the post-war debate (see page 4) a whole series of theories were put forward to try to explain these changes within society. Marxist historians maintained that such social changes were mainly the consequence of shifts in economic relationships at all levels. Revisionist historians, on the other hand, considered that changes in political relationships among the elites were the major influence on the social structure. However, many historians were not convinced by either of these two major explanations of social change. They stressed the importance of religious change, the variations in population levels, and the effect of inflation in creating movements within and between social groups.

a) Marxist Theories of Social Change

There was considerable disagreement among Marxist historians over the explanation of the emergence of what they saw as an increasingly capitalistic society during the first half of the sixteenth century. The most orthodox theory was that there was a complete change in agricultural relationships. This was seen as starting during the feudal crisis, which had been caused by a breakdown in relations between landlords and peasant farmers. During the fifteenth century the English peasant communities had been strong enough to free themselves from labour services and other feudal dues, so that they had much greater control over their land and paid lower rents. In the sixteenth century the landlords were able to use their political power to push up the level of rents, and so begin to force the peasants off their land. Former peasant smallholdings were consolidated into larger farms, which were either leased out or kept by the landowner.

In both cases the land was farmed commercially, using the now land-less, former peasantry as labour. This, it is maintained, created a new, exploitive capitalistic relationship between landholders and landless labourers. It was this loss of independence that led to resentment and class conflict between wage labourers and landowners.

An alternative theory for the emergence of a capitalistic society is 'the growth of world trade'. This was seen as making labour relation-ships based on market forces more attractive to both landlords and peasants than the old feudal ones. Estate owners found it more prof-itable to produce food for sale, and to work their land by wage labour. Some peasant smallholders either used the situation to acquire more land and become yeomen, selling food for the market, or to give up their land altogether to work for wages. However, many peasants preferred to retain their smallholdings and to remain self-sufficient. It was this that caused tensions between a self-sufficient peasant economy and market forces. At the same time it created class conflict between the peasant smallholders and the new commercial farmers.

Another explanation stressed the importance of the spread of urban and industrial relationships, already based on wage labour, into the countryside. This was seen as an essential step towards a capital-istic society. Since the thirteenth century merchants and industrialists had been transferring some of the textile trades from the towns into the countryside, where they could employ cheaper peasant labour. This created tensions between urban and rural communities. At the same time they were buying country estates and introducing more commercial techniques using wage labour. These methods were adopted by many of their rural neighbours, and so commercial farming spread, particularly near towns. This growing commercial group created a new class, the 'bourgeoisie'. The Crown favoured the bourgeoisie because it could use its members to staff the growing state bureaucracy, and so reduce the influence of the aristocracy. This created class conflict between the bourgeoisie and the aristocracy, which the Crown used to strengthen its own position. At the same time there was growing class conflict between the expanding indus-trial labour force and its employers.

These various Marxist theories of social change saw the emer-gence of capitalistic relationships causing class conflict at all levels within English society. This was once thought to be the major cause of the widespread popular discontent in the middle of the sixteenth century which led to peasant rebellions in 1549. However, many historians, even Marxists, are now very doubtful whether there is any evidence of class, let alone class conflict, in the sixteenth century. Another idea central to Marxist theories was of the 'peas-antry' being driven from the land by avaricious landlords. Here again this notion is no longer widely accepted, and it is thought that the 'disappearnce of the peasantry' was due to increased commercial competition and economic change.

b) Revisionist Theories of Social Change

Revisionist historians, while they agreed that society began to change after the feudal crisis, offer an entirely different explanation of events. For them, social restructuring was caused by shifts in political relationships among the landed and ruling elites caused by the rise of the State. The feudal anarchy caused by quarrels among the aristocracy had enabled western European monarchs to gain greater authority through the support of the bulk of the population. This meant that the State was able to centralise political power, and reduce the influence of the aristocracy in the provinces. Consequently, it is maintained, the aristocracy and the other landed elites became dependent on the State for support. To maintain their social, political and economic position they had to rely upon royal patronage to give them offices at Court, in the government or in the army. Social changes developing in England during the first half of the sixteenth century were seen in terms of an elitist power struggle. Revisionist historians totally disagreed with Marxist and other historians who maintained that the gentry rose because of their ability to exploit the favourable economic conditions of the early part of the sixteenth century. For them, it was the ability to obtain offices from the Crown that led to the rise of the gentry. They see the emergence of men like Somerset and Northumberland resulting entirely from their success in gaining royal favour, at the expense of established aristocratic families such as the Howards, the Dukes of Norfolk. The fall of Somerset in 1549, and the ensuing rivalry between the conservatives and the reformers, was interpreted as part of the elite power struggle.

Many historians have not been convinced by this revisionist explanation of social change. They have considered that the so-called power struggle was just part of the normal rise and fall of aristocratic and gentry families, and they have seen no evidence that the early Tudors favoured new families in preference to the ancient aristocracy. It has also been pointed out that this theory has the great weakness that it does not account for social change among the rest of the population.

c) Religion and Social Change

The Reformation used to be seen as being particularly important in the process of social change. It was considered that the break from Rome and the introduction of Protestantism (see page 77) was important in promoting the spread of individualism, capitalism and competition. It was suggested that many members of the elites and commercial groups adopted moderate Protestantism so that they could benefit from the growth of market forces. Equally the seizure of church lands was seen as helping the elites to build up their wealth, and to recover from the losses resulting from the breakdown of the late medieval economy. It was claimed that the Western Rebellion of 1549 (see page 86) provides evidence of such developments. Certainly, the rebels were hostile towards the local gentry who, they claimed, were using the Reformation to enrich themselves. At the same time, the adoption of Lutheran and Calvinist ideas during the reign of Edward VI was seen as introducing the Protestant work ethic, with its stress on thrift, sobriety and hard work, into England. This, along with the attack upon superstitious rituals and Holy Days, was considered to have begun to break down the seasonal life of the lower orders. It was the threat to their lifestyle as much as their attachment to the Catholic religion, it was suggested, that provoked the rebels in the West Country in 1549. However, there now is considerable scepticism about the whole concept of the Protestant work ethic. It is also pointed out that the Catholic rural and urban elites were just as adept at acquiring confiscated monastic property and money-making as their Protestant counterparts. In any case, the apparent religious apathy of the majority of the population makes it difficult to decide whether religion had any long-term or short-term effects on social change.

d) Population and Social Change

Many social and economic historians have not been completely convinced by any of these general theories of social change. They have considered that variations in the levels of population and the consequent inflation, or deflation, were the major influence on the social structure. For them the deflationary period following the Black Death of 1349, caused by falling population levels, created a period of lower order prosperity. Many smallholders gave up their land and became wage labourers in order to benefit from the high wage levels. On the other hand, deflation caused economic problems for the landed elites (see page 14). However, when the population began to recover at the beginning of the sixteenth century the situation was reversed. Landowners now began to benefit from increased prices caused by inflation. At the same time they were able to push up rents because more people were looking for land to rent. This in turn has been seen as forcing many of the remaining husbandmen and cottagers from the land because they could not afford the higher rents. As more people were available for work, wages did not increase at the same rate as prices. Consequently the living standards of both smallholders and wage labourers fell, while most of the elites were prospering. It has been suggested that it was the effect of this change that was being fully felt by 1549, and was a cause of the popular unrest.

Although these theories still remain a good starting point for thinking about social change in early modern England, they, like all general theories, are now considered to be far too restrictive.

Continued research, particularly at local level, has revealed an English society too varied to be explained by any theory. There were great differences between regions, counties and even neighbouring villages. Equally, convenient labels such as 'capitalism' or 'bourgeioise' are no longer thought appropriate for the sixteenth century. Similarly, concepts such as 'the Protestant work ethic' are thought to be equally inappropriate. While society at all levels was becoming more fluid and individualistic, and there was an increase in commercialisation and competition, this is no longer seen as a cause of conflict. Indeed, it can be maintained that popular discontent was always close to the surface in pre-industrial societies where so many people lived near the poverty line. Only in times of acute hardship, such as famine or widespread unemployment, did grievances erupt into violence. So it might well be said that the mid-century problems were more economic than social (see Chapter 6).

2 Social Models

> **KEY ISSUES** What are the main differences between the late-medieval and the mid-Tudor social models? How did social and geographical mobility contribute towards social change? How useful are social models? What are their advantages and disadvantages?

English society underwent an important period of evolution between 1350 and 1550. Mid-sixteenth-century society is seen as being more competitive and individualistic than it had been during the Middle Ages. Even so, it is considered that it was still overwhelmingly rural, and retained many of the characteristics of feudal society (see page 19). To clarify the social complexities in early modern England, post-war historians constructed various social models. Two of these helped to measure the nature and extent of the changes taking place over these 200 years. One of the most important signs of change is thought to be the amount of social mobility existing between the various groups. Therefore it is important to understand the nature of the social mobility which existed in late medieval society.

a) The Late-Medieval Social Model

The late-medieval social model was seen as being a pyramid of status based on land ownership, which contained 95 per cent of the population. At the top was the king, who was the main landowner. Below him came the nobility (dukes, marquesses, earls, viscounts and barons), which was made up of about 60 families. These great estate owners, along with their wives and families, formed the top rank of society. A nobleman's position within the aristocratic elite depended upon the amount of land he possessed. Smaller landowners, many of whom were younger sons and new entrants, formed a second tier below the nobility. Under them came the yeomen, defined as those who owned land worth at least 40 shillings a year. At the bottom was the great bulk of the population, the peasantry, who rented smallholdings on the manors of the elites. The remaining five per cent of the population consisted of the clergy and town dwellers. The clerical hierarchy depended not on birth and size of estates, but on the importance of the position held. At the top was the Archbishop of Canterbury, with the parish clergy at the bottom. Towns are seen as being outside the rural feudal structure, with populations that were more individualistic and educated than that of the surrounding countryside. Status in the urban hierarchy was based on wealth, and at the top were rich merchants and the master craftsmen of the guilds. Below them came the shopkeepers, small traders, journeymen and apprentices. The great mass of town society was made up of servants, labourers and the poor.

b) Late-Medieval Social Mobility

Social mobility, although limited, is thought to have taken place within and between these three hierarchies. Members of the aristocratic elite were socially equal to each other and to the king. Apart from the hereditary nobility the only other title among the group was that of knight. This was a military distinction, and, theoretically, was only granted by the king, a feudal superior, or a military commander on the battlefield as a mark of bravery. However, it became normal for the king to reward members of the elites with knighthoods for a variety of non-military services. Educational opportunities were limited. Boys were given a military training, and girls were taught the art of household management. Successful marriage alliances were seen as a major means of upward social mobility. Daughters were frequently married off very early (although not before the age of seven) to secure military, political or financial alliances. Only the eldest son could inherit the family estates, so younger sons had to seek alternative careers. A minority entered the Church or one of the monastic orders, where they could achieve high office either in England or on the continent. As the clergy were the only educated section of society, successful clerics often obtained important offices in the royal government. A religious career in one of the orders of nuns also offered an alternative to marriage for the daughters of the elites. War was the predominant interest of the elites. Family fortunes could be recouped, and penniless younger sons could start their careers from the ransoms, booty and glory to be won in a successful military campaign.

For the remainder of rural society, social mobility was much more limited. Among the yeomen there was a certain amount of upward mobility into the lower ranks of the elites through success in farming, trade, industry, war or marriage. However, the great majority of the peasantry were not free. Legally they were serfs, and were the property of the landowner on whose manor they lived. This meant that they were not allowed to leave without the permission of the lord of the manor, and so there was little opportunity for either social or geographical mobility. As in the case of the elites it was normally only the eldest son who could inherit the family smallholding. Younger children became servants in husbandry, either at home or on neighbouring farms, until a vacant holding became available, and they could get married. This meant that most of the rural population lived and died within a few miles of where they were born. A few fortunate younger children, whose parents had enough money to buy permission for them to leave the manor, were able to gain upward social mobility. Some went into the Church or monastic orders, while others became apprenticed in one of the craft industries in the towns.

Urban societies, with the exception of London, were small and inward looking. Strong commercial rivalry meant that outsiders were regarded with suspicion, and so found it difficult to establish themselves. As only the eldest son inherited the family business, even younger children found it very difficult to break into the close-knit ruling circles. However, like the Church, towns offered a means of social mobility within an otherwise stable rural hierarchy. For the lower orders the towns provided some opportunity for geographical mobility, and the chance of improved social status for the lucky few. Only for those in, or reaching, the town ruling circles was considerable social mobility possible. Wealthy merchants were able to buy country estates and merge into the landed elites, or to marry their sons and daughters into noble or aristocratic families.

c) The Mid-Tudor Social Model

The events taking place in the late fourteenth and fifteenth centuries, however interpreted, were seen as causing a quickening in the pace of social change. However, it was considered that there had been little structural change by the middle of the sixteenth century. The three social hierarchies stayed broadly unaltered in size and their relationship to each other. The late medieval economic decline was seen as adversely affecting both the towns and the Church in economic terms, but having no impact upon their social structure. It was rural society that is considered to have been changed both economically and socially.

i) The Rural Elites
The great landowners, both lay and ecclesiastical, lost economic and political power to the Crown. In addition, the nobility forfeited their

military independence. The social effect of this change was to make the king the social superior of the elites, instead of their equal. Under the early Tudors such superiority was reinforced by the concept of the monarch being the father of the nation to whom all subjects owed obedience (see page 9). Another consequence of the economic decline of the great landowners was that during the fifteenth century some of them had to sell part of their land, and lease out much of the remainder on long leases of up to 99 years. The immediate impact of this was the temporary lowering of the social prestige of the nobility. They could no longer afford to maintain their great households, and service to the Crown became more attractive to the ambitious among the lesser elites. Likewise, the sale and leasing out of the great estates created a very active land market, which widened the availability of land. This was the beginning of the rise of the gentry. The old elite became divided into two parts. Aristocratic society – the nobles and their immediate families – ranked below the monarch. Their younger children, their families and their descendants evolved into a lesser elite – the gentry – below the aristocracy. There were three ranks in this new social group. At the top were the knights. The title had partially lost its old military significance, although it still was not hereditary. Knights could be created for a variety of reasons, yet the title increasingly came to denote a landowner with estates worth at least £100 a year. Next in rank to the knight was the esquire – a title given to the children of knights and their descendants. The lowest rank among the gentry was the gentleman – a title given to the younger children of esquires and their descendants.

All the existing means of social mobility remained the same. The major change was that there had been a significant redistribution of land to the new gentry. When prices and rents began to rise after 1500 it was the gentry who benefited from such increases, and from the improving industrial and commercial conditions. The aristocracy were unable to reap any real profit from their estates until the long leases ran out towards the end of the sixteenth century and they were able to repossess their land. Another highly significant development which is considered to have altered the pattern of social mobility, particularly among the elites, was the spread of the Renaissance and Christian humanism in England at the end of the fifteenth century. These Renaissance ideas are seen as weakening the influence of the Church. Apart from causing a growth in anti-clericalism by attacking the wealth and abuses in the Church, Renaissance thought encouraged the spread of secular education. Previously a clerical career was seen as not just an opportunity to obtain high office in the Church, but as a means of gaining important governmental positions. The spread of Christian humanism, with its emphasis on education for the laity, promoted the universities, the legal Inns of Court and secular schools as an alternative for political careerists. Thomas Wolsey, the son of a Suffolk cattle dealer who rose to become a cardinal, the

Archbishop of York, and Lord Chancellor under Henry VIII, is seen as the last of the great English clerical careerists. His successors, such as Thomas Cromwell and William Cecil, came to power through a university and legal education. Increasingly this became the route taken by those aspiring to a political and administrative career.

ii) The Rural Lower Orders

Equally significant changes were taking place among the rural lower orders. The decline in economic and political power among the great landowners is considered to have brought about the disappearance of serfdom and labour services in England during the fifteenth century. All the peasantry were now theoretically free (although there were still serfs in some parts of England until the end of the sixteenth century), and so could move about the country as they chose. This is seen as ending, or at least drastically altering, the structure of peasant society. Peasant smallholders were generally described as husbandmen. Customary tenures were being replaced by a new form of tenancy for the lifetime of the holder called copyhold, for which rent was paid in cash. Many of the former peasants took advantage of the availability of land and amassed holdings of some 200 acres or more. They became commercial farmers, and joined the ranks of the yeomen. Now that the new copyhold tenancies no longer carried the stigma of being unfree, many of the former yeomen and new gentry were also prepared to acquire this type of land. However, many husbandmen preferred to remain self-sufficient smallholders, with about 30-40 acres of land. At the same time some improved their position by acquiring enough land to become self-sufficient. Others preferred to continue to supplement the produce of their smallholdings by working for wages on the commercial farms and in rural industry. A significant number decided to take advantage of the higher wage levels created by the fall in the size of the labour force, and abandon their land to work full-time for wages. All the existing routes of social mobility remained the same, but, because the lower orders now enjoyed much greater geographical mobility, many more people could take advantage of them.

d) The Difficulties of Using Social Models

Although these models do help to give a broad picture of the social structure and the process of social change, they, like the general theories, are too vague and sweeping. This means that they tend to obscure the wide local differences that exited within society, and the full range of the changes that were taking place. Recent research has revealed considerable variations at all levels of society. Not all the aristocracy were in decline, neither were all the gentry rising. Indeed, downward mobility was just as prevalent among the gentry as among the aristocracy. The idea of a static medieval peasant population with the vast majority of families living for generations in the same village has been disproved, although it is true that the early Tudor lower orders were even more geographically mobile. Similarly, it has been shown that not all towns were in economic decline. Some, particularly London, were prospering, while others were passing into obscurity. It is important to stress the localised nature of early Tudor society. The emphasis is now put on the importance and differences between counties and even neighbouring villages. There was a keen sense of local loyalty and interference by the central government was resisted. Tudor MPs were much more interested in matters relating to their own locality than in national events. Similarly, local societies had their own loyalties and interests, which were not necessarily the same as those of their social counterparts elsewhere in the country.

3 Tudor Society in 1522

> **KEY ISSUES** Why are the 1522 Muster Certificates so useful to historians? How far does the picture of society that they reveal confirm or contradict historians' views on social change since the late Middle Ages?

One way of overcoming these problems is to look at how Tudors themselves saw their own society. Fortunately, a remarkably full picture of English society is provided in 1522. In that year the Privy Council ordered a survey to be made of all men fit for military service. At the same time the government used the survey to inquire into the value of land and movable goods held by everyone in the country in order to draw up new tax schedules. As a result, the survey provides the most comprehensive census of English society between the Domesday Book of 1086 and the first census in 1801. Unfortunately, the muster returns for 1522 have not survived for all counties. However, sufficient numbers remain for historians to use them over the past 20 years to analyse the state of early Tudor society.

The picture that emerges from the muster returns is of considerable underlying continuity, but there are clear signs of increasing commercialisation by the 1520s. England was still predominantly rural, and most of the population still lived in small villages. The Church continued to be the largest single holder of land, and there is little evidence of any marked changes in the composition of urban society. However, although the villages were mainly made up of communities of husbandmen, most of them had at least one (and usually more) commercial farmer, or yeoman. It is also clear that the number of servants in husbandry and labourers had increased noticeably, and it is estimated that 40 per cent of the lower orders were wage-earners. The rise of the gentry as a group was clearly well advanced. By the 1520s they held some 30 per cent of the manors, and were the leaseholders of many more.

a) Shellingford in 1522

The Muster Certificate for Shellingford, 1522

1   *The value of lands & property there*
     The Abbot of Abingdon is chief lord there & his lands are in value by
     the year over all charges £40 0s 0d
     Thomas Unton Gent. in lands 6s 8d
5   John Elyotte in lands 5s 8d
     Sir William Craddock Clerk is parson there & his parsonage is in
     value by the year over all charges £13 0s 0d

     The value of goods & other movable property there
10   John Wyse senior householder £22 0s 0d
     John White servant 12s 0d
     John Yate h. £5 0s 0d
     Robert Barteley servant £1 0s 0d
     Thomas Abday h. £7 0s 0d
15   Thomas Seuernake £2 0s 0d
     John Bowell h. £4 0s 0d
     William Badnoll h. £13 6s 8d
     Robert Ryve servant £1 6s 8d
     Thomas Carter servant £1 0s 0d
20   William Browne h. £1 0s 0d
     John Cowley h. £2 0s 0d
     John Chirchey h. £3 0s 0d
     John Tayllor h. £12 0s 0d
     William Yate h. £14 0s 0d
25   Thomas Yate his son £2 0s 0d
     William Somner servant 10s 0d
     Harry Harne h. £1 0s 0d
     Phillippe Smythe h. £2 0s 0d
     John Smythe h. £5 6s 8d
30   Margory Chirche widow £1 0s 0d
     Julyan Chirche widow £1 0s 0d
     Margett of Acris widow 10s 0d

Shellingford was a small village in Berkshire and shows many of the characteristics of a rural community in the 1520s. The local abbey still owned the manor. There are two small pieces of freehold land, one held by a member of the local gentry, the other by a husbandman from the nearby village of Stanford. The parson held a large piece of land attached to the parsonage. What is not shown is that Thomas Unton's brother Alexander Unton, gentleman, had held the lease of the manor from the abbey for 33 years from 1508. None of these people lived in the village; the residents are listed under the goods and property valuation. All of those marked 'householder' or with 'h.' occupied a farm or smallholding. It has been estimated that in 1522 anyone with goods worth more than nine pounds was a yeoman, and that any husbandman with goods worth between five pounds and nine pounds was likely to be self-sufficient. Clearly, by 1522 there was already a wide disparity in wealth between the villagers.

4 The Impact of the English Reformation on Mid-Tudor Society

> **KEY ISSUES** Why was a shortage of land causing growing competition within society? To what extent could the English Reformation be said to have been politically and socially motivated? What impact did the redistribution of church lands have on elite society? How did these changes effect the rest of society?

Although the picture of the shape of English society in the 1520s is reasonably clear, lack of evidence makes it much more difficult to decide how far it had developed by the middle of the century. There seems to be little sign that the increase in population had begun to affect the living standards of the lower orders by the1520s. There were still copyholds available at a reasonable rent, and prices had not risen sufficiently to outstrip wages in a significant way. However, it is considered that the buoyant land market of the fifteenth century was beginning to become static, and that demand for land among the elites had begun to exceed the supply. There is seen to be growing rivalry between the aristocracy, gentry and yeomen for land. Such competition was not caused just by the increased numbers of gentry and yeomen. By the 1520s commercial opportunities were improving for landowners. Many of the great estate owners, whose land was still tied up with long leases, wished to obtain additional land so that they could take advantage of the upturn in the economy. In addition, leaseholders were anxious to convert their leases into freehold, or to obtain other land, before the term of their tenancy ran out. This situation is seen as being potentially dangerous for the Crown, as it was causing instability among the elites.

a) The Redistribution of Church Property

Some historians consider that there is a clear link between this situation and the English Reformation. They suggest that Henry VIII embarked on the spoliation of the English Church in order to satisfy the growing land hunger among the elites. It was vital to the Crown that it should keep the active support of the elites. Clearly, it was in the interests of both the parties to re-distribute the wealth of the English Church between them. Equally, outside interference in English affairs by the papacy was resented by both the monarchy and the elites. Hence the subordination the English Church to the Crown through the royal supremacy was a popular move. It has been pointed out that in order to maintain this claim reformers and conservatives among the elites were firm supporters of the royal supremacy. Furthermore it is indicated that Catholics were just as active in acquiring church property as were the Protestants. Such an interpretation, it is suggested, is confirmed by the complete solidarity among the Protestant and Catholic elites in resisting Mary I's attempts in 1554 to restore all church lands sold after 1536.

By 1553, largely as a result of the closure of the monasteries, church lands with an annual value of about five million pounds had passed into lay ownership. This was the largest redistribution of land since the Norman Conquest and was, clearly, to have a considerable impact on the structure of elite society. In north Berkshire in 1536 the Church held 51 per cent of the freehold land, 33 per cent of which belonged to the monasteries. Of the remainder the gentry held 34 per cent, the King 8 per cent and the aristocracy 7 per cent. By 1553 the gentry held 51 per cent, while the Crown and the aristocracy had both increased their share slightly. Such figures vary from county to county, but it is clear that the gentry were the major beneficiaries of the sale of monastic land. However, it must be remembered that in many cases the gentry were already the leasees of the estates that they purchased. For example, the manor of Shellingford (see page 115) was surrendered to the Crown by Abingdon Abbey in 1538. In 1539 the King granted the estate to the leasee, Alexander Unton, at a ground rent of £4 13s. 4d per year. Unton also bought the neighbouring royal manor of Hatford in 1544. The immediate effect of the sale of church land seems to have been that the existing gentry consolidated their position by converting leaseholds into permanent possession, or by acquiring additional estates. The same applies to the nobility, who added church land to their already considerable territorial holdings. By 1558 only a small amount of land appears to have passed into the possession of new owners from the towns or industry. However, there is plenty of evidence to show that in the Home Counties, particularly in Kent, London merchants were very active in the land market even at this stage.

b) The Effects of Secularisation

It appears that by 1558 the secularisation of ecclesiastical property had had very little effect on the structure of elite society. With the exception of the immediate vicinity of London, the land had gone to consolidate the position of the existing aristocracy and gentry. The

Church had lost a great deal of wealth and power. In due course this was to lower the prestige of the clergy and make a clerical career less attractive to the younger sons of the elites, but this was not apparent in 1558. It is true that the opportunity for a monastic career in England had vanished, but with a buoyant land market and a growing variety of other career opportunities, it is doubtful that this was regarded by the elites as a serious loss. However, while other career routes for younger sons remained the same, for daughters, the disappearance of the nunneries left marriage as the only possible opening.

For the remainder of society the redistribution of land had little, or no, immediate effect. The losses sustained by the Church left the clerical hierarchy unchanged, apart from the disappearance of abbots, which lessened ecclesiastical influence in the House of Lords. While many of the dispossesed monks and friars joined the ranks of the parish clergy, many nuns left to enter convents on the continent. The urban hierarchies remained unaltered. Some of the town elites enhanced their position by purchasing blocks of ecclesiastical urban property, while a few had succeeded in moving into the ranks of the gentry through buying a country estate. This provided some openings for new entrants into the town ruling bodies, but otherwise the opportunities for upward social mobility remained the same. For the great majority – the rural and urban non-elites – the redistribution of land had no effect whatsoever. All that happened was that they became the tenants of new landowners. In the past it has been suggested that the new owners were more rapacious than the old ecclesiastical landlords. This view has now been rejected. It is considered that church-owned land and property had been just as vigorously exploited as that held by the laity. In any case, as many of the church estates passed into the ownership of former leasees, it is unlikely that there was any noticeable change in management.

5 Mid-Tudor Society

> **KEY ISSUE** How well do historians' reconstructions of mid-Tudor society conform to the views of Sir Thomas Smith?

By 1558 it appears that there had been little further alteration to the social structure at any level. Changes to elite society since the late Middle Ages had progressed and been consolidated. The monarchy had established its position of social and political superiority. By recouping their economic losses the nobility and aristocracy had consolidated themselves as the major landowning group below the King. The gentry had established themselves as the rank immediately below the aristocracy. Yeomen were recognised as the most important landowners below the gentry. The urban and clerical hierarchies remained unchanged. Self-sufficient husbandmen were still the most numerous group in the rural communities. The number of wage-earners had increased and they were forming a growing rural and urban proletariat.

a) Contemporary Views of Mid-Tudor Society

At this point it must be asked whether historians are justified in creating such a picture of the early English social hierarchy. For this purpose it is necessary to compare their reconstruction with a contemporary view of mid-Tudor society. In 1565 Sir Thomas Smith, who had been Secretary of State under Somerset, wrote the book *The Commonwealth of England* (*De Republica Anglorum*), in which he described English society as he saw it. It must be remembered that this was an elite viewpoint, and it is not possible to be sure of the author's motives for writing the book. It may be that he was depicting society as he thought it should be, rather than showing it as it actually existed in the middle of the sixteenth century. Again he might, like the Norfolk rebels (see page 125), be nostalgically looking back to a society which he thought was vanishing.

1   Of the first part of Gentlemen of England, called *nobilitas major*. ... In England no man is created baron, except he may dispend of yearly revenue one thousand pounds ...
   Of the second sort of Gentlemen, which may be called *nobilitas minor* ...
5   No man is a knight by succession, not the king or prince ... knights therefore be not born but made ... Esquires be all those which bear arms ... these be taken for no distinct order of the commonwealth, but do go with the residue of gentlemen ... Gentlemen be those whom their blood and race doth make noble and known ... For whosoever studieth the
10 laws of the realm, who studieth in the Universities ... and to be short, who can live idly and without manual labour, and will bear the port, charge and countenance of a gentleman, he shall be called master ...
   Those whom we call yeomen, next unto the nobility, knights and squires ... is a freeman born English, and may dispend of his own free
15 land in yearly revenue to the sum of 40s. sterling ...
   The fourth sort or class amongst us, is of those ... day labourers, poor husbandmen, yea merchants or retailers which have no free land, copy-holders and all artificers [wage labourers] ... These have no voice nor authority in our commonwealth, and no account is made of them, but
20 only to be ruled.

6 A Social Crisis, 1547-58?

> **KEY ISSUES** Is there any evidence that rivalry among the elites amounted to a social crisis? Why is it now thought that lower order discontent was more economic than social? How far is this idea supported by the demands of the rebels in Norfolk?

In the past it has been suggested that the popular rebellions and the elite power struggle in 1549 indicate a social crisis at all levels of society. In view of the apparent stability in all the social hierarchies this conclusion is no longer considered valid. In social terms neither the urban nor the clerical hierarchies displayed any signs of pressure. The clergy and urban elites appear to have supported the Crown and the maintenance of order and stability. Furthermore, no drastic change can be seen in the pattern of social development among the lower orders. After 200 years of transition English society appears to have reached a firm platform, which was to act as a springboard for the next phase of transformation.

a) Conflict Among the Elites?

A number of suggestions have been put forward to support the contention that competition among the elites had reached crisis point by the middle of the sixteenth century. One of these is that the numbers of the elites were increasing more rapidly than the rest of the population, particularly after 1500, because the economic conditions favoured them. For this reason women in the elite groups were able to marry earlier, on average at the age of 20-21, while women in the lower orders were marrying later, on average at the age of 27-28. This meant that elite families were having 4.5 children on average, while the non-elites were only averaging 2 children. There certainly is evidence to show that the size of elite families was increasing by the middle of the century. For example, William Hyde esquire of Denchworth in Berkshire, who died in 1557, had thirteen surviving children, and his eldest son had ten children. Even so, doubts are expressed about what effect such developments would have had by 1558. In 1500 it has been estimated that there were 55 nobles, 500 knights, 800 esquires and 5,000 gentlemen. By 1550 there were still 55 nobles and 500 knights. Although the numbers of esquires and gentlemen had risen, it is thought unlikely that the rate of increase greatly exceeded the general population growth of one per cent per year. It is now considered that, given the surplus of monastic land, any increases in numbers would have been insufficient to cause any real problems. However, it is thought that large elite families, and a growing shortage of land for purchase, may well have been one of the causes of the social tensions building up by 1600.

It is still thought that there were signs of increasing competition between the rising gentry and the aristocracy. However, this is seen in terms of traditional elite rivalry for land and power rather than in terms of the arguments put forward in the Marxist-Revisionist debate. It has been estimated that in 1500 the nobility had an average income of £1,000 a year compared with £130 for knights, £58 for esquires and £14 for gentlemen. There are no similar estimates for the middle of the century, but it is thought that the incomes for all four groups increased at approximately the same rate. However, there were wide disparities of wealth within each rank. For example, by 1548 Somerset had an income of £7,400 a year from his estates, and a further £5,000 annually from public funds for his office as Lord Protector. Much of his personal wealth came from his success in acquiring ecclesiastical property. Fellow members of the Privy Council – Northumberland, Herbert, Paget, Russell, Rich and Wriothesley – had similarly enriched themselves with church lands. Other aristocratic incomes varied from £3,000–4,000 a year down to a few hundred pounds a year. Former gentry families like the Seymours and Dudleys, through a combination of military careers, royal favour, public office and the seizure of church lands, had risen rapidly to the top ranks of the social hierarchy. Such success was exceptional, and must be seen merely as part of the traditional pattern of rising and falling fortune among the elites. Former suggestions that Henry VII and Henry VIII deliberately tried to change the social composition of the aristocracy by promoting new families at the expense of the ancient nobility are now thought to be unfounded. At a county level, fortune among the gentry was just as varied. In north Berkshire three of the established knightly families, the Fettiplaces, Essexes and Norreys, were the most successful in accumulating church land. By 1553 the Fettiplaces had increased their landed income only marginally from £182 a year in 1522 to £184, the Essexes' income had risen from £160 to £238, and the Norreys' land in Berkshire actually fell in value from £142 to £113, but they had been acquiring land in neighbouring Oxfordshire. Another family, the Yates, who were merchants on the fringes of gentility in 1522, increased their landholding from £22 to £122 over the same period. Most of the north Berkshire gentry had not acquired church lands by 1553. For example, the ancient family of Pusey, with one manor worth £3 in 1522, still had the same amount of land in 1553.

i) A 'Wheel of Fortune'

Success or failure was by no means dependent upon the ability to buy church property. Old noble families such as the Percys, Nevilles and Poles, had fallen through royal disfavour. Others, like the Howards, survived the displeasure of the monarchy to rise again. The Brandon family, which had risen rapidly through royal marriage, fell back into obscurity because it failed to produce male heirs. Families such as the Spencers were establishing themselves through their success in sheep raising and other commercial enterprises. Among the higher clergy, men like Cranmer, Gardiner and Pole continued to exercise considerable political influence, although not on the scale of Thomas Wolsey earlier in the century. Among the lesser elites a gap was starting to develop. Some of the 'greater' gentry began to rival the aristocracy for wealth, while many of the 'parish' gentry became barely distinguishable from yeomen. Again, this is regarded as part of the traditional pattern of success or failure – a 'wheel of fortune' with families rising, falling or stagnating.

The subsequent histories of the five Berkshire families already mentioned are good examples in the variations in fortune. The Fettiplaces had enjoyed considerable royal favour through offices at Court until the middle of the century. However, by then they were heavily in debt, and tried to recoup their losses by purchasing land so that they could take advantage of the expected inflation in land values. At the same time they supported Somerset in his rise to power and, after his execution in 1552, they fell out of Court favour. During the second half of the sixteenth century they were forced to sell more of their estates and never regained their former eminence. The long-established Essex family also speculated in land, with even less success, and they had become bankrupt by 1600. In contrast the Norreys were very successful in their land dealings, and, through royal favour under Elizabeth, they rose to become the Earls of Banbury in Oxfordshire. In spite of being strong Catholic sympathisers, the Yates family consolidated their position in the ranks of the gentry. The Pusey family demonstrated that in the favourable economic conditions it was possible to prosper even without acquiring additional land. In 1522 Thomas Pusey's wealth had been estimated at £8. When his grandson Philip died in 1573 he left £238 in his will. This represents an increase of over 2,800 per cent in 50 years, whereas the rate of inflation was only 200 per cent over the same period.

ii) Assessment

With a buoyant land market, there appears to be little reason to suppose that there was sufficient social rivalry between the gentry and the aristocracy to amount to a crisis. There was competition, but there were ample opportunities for advancement for the enterprising individual. In any case, it is difficult to see why there should be serious antagonism between the gentry and the aristocracy at this juncture. Most of the gentry were members of well-established families descended from, and related by marriage to, the aristocracy. In 1558 the elites still appear to have been a closely-knit group, bound together by their belief in their social superiority and their right to rule by birth.

b) Lower-Order Discontent?

If there was social conflict and crisis in mid-Tudor England, the popular uprisings of 1549 appear to suggest that it was caused by problems among the lower orders. The difficulty is to decide whether the problems were caused by social tensions. Lower order society had been evolving steadily since the end of the Middle Ages. Its structure had been created by the opportunities offered by the improved economic conditions of the fifteenth century. Thus it resulted from competition among the non-elites themselves and had not been imposed on them by the elites. No reason is seen why the comparatively stable, non-elite society of the 1520s should have radically altered by the middle of the century. The problem is considered to lie in the economic conditions, which no longer favoured the lower orders. Rising population and inflation brought prosperity to the elites, but eroded the standard of living for the masses – a situation on which R.H. Tawney, one of the early pioneering social historians, commented in 1912: 'Villeinage [serfdom] ceases but the poor laws begin'.

i) Population Pressure

There is ample evidence to support such an interpretation of the problems in 1549. It is estimated that the population was rising at the rate of one per cent per year, and possibly faster, up to the middle of the century. This would have meant that the fairly comfortable population level of 2.3 million in 1522 may well have reached some three million by 1550. This, it is thought, might well have put a strain on food production and created a Malthusian crisis, which was made worse by the harvest failure in 1549. The greater number of people enabled landowners to push up the level of rents, while employers were able to keep down wages. In contrast, inflation, which is estimated to have run at four per cent per year over the whole country, was compounded by the debasements of the coinage in the 1540s (see page 37) and may well have reached over 200 per cent by 1550. For the growing number of cloth workers the situation was made worse by the decline of the Antwerp cloth market (see pages 151-2), resulting in heavy job losses in the country's largest industry. Furthermore, the comparative lack of popular unrest in the 1550s can be explained by heavy mortality caused by severe epidemics of plague and 'sweating sickness' in 1551 and 1552, and of influenza between 1556 and 1558, which relieved population pressure.

ii) Social Conflict?

It was once thought that the popular rebellions of 1549 offered clear proof of social conflict directed particularly against the gentry. It is true that in the West Country and in Norfolk the rebels were antagonistic towards the local gentry. The Privy Council described both uprisings as social conflict which threatened to undermine the whole fabric of society. However, historians now regard such statements as government propaganda intended to unite the elites behind an increasingly unpopular administration. Much of the resentment towards the gentry centred on the accusation that they were using the Reformation to enrich themselves and to exploit their tenants. But, as it has been suggested, there is little reason to see why the sale of church lands should have had any great effect upon the tenants. Another major cause of resentment was that the rebels, like the government, mistak-

enly blamed enclosure for the adverse economic situation. It is difficult to see how this could have had an immediate effect in 1549. The
great bulk of enclosures had taken place before 1520, and most of it
was in the Midlands, where there were no popular uprisings. Clearly
enclosure did have a social effect in altering the pattern of community
life in the villages, but it was part of the changes that had been in
progress since the end of the fourteenth century. In any case, much of
the enclosure had been carried out by mutual consent among the
husbandmen, to improve agricultural production.

iii) Adverse Economic Conditions
It is now considered that such apparent social conflict was really the
reaction of the masses to economic hardship. It is estimated that
during the sixteenth century at least 50 per cent of the rural and
urban non-elites lived on, or below, the poverty line – even in good
years. Discontent, therefore, was always just below the surface, and
broke into revolt at times of widespread unemployment and food
shortages, such as in 1549. On such occasions the ruling elites were
always accused of economic and political exploitation. Of course, it
can be argued that this was a form of social crisis because the elites
were responsible for maintaining a social structure which placed
them in a highly privileged position. However, it must be remembered that the social structure of the rural lower orders in the mid-
sixteenth century had been created when they had had the economic
advantage in the fifteenth century. It is suggested that the rural rebels
were largely illiterate and inarticulate, and relied on rumour and
hearsay to explain problems which they did not understand. For this
reason local issues and grievances became of paramount importance,
and the past became a vanished 'golden age' of prosperity to which
they wished to return. Consequently, many of the grievances of such
uprisings belonged more to a 'folk memory' of past events rather than
to current issues. Kett's rebellion in Norfolk is a good example of this
interpretation.

iv) Kett's Rebellion, 1549
East Anglia was the most densely populated and highly industrialised
part of the country. Norwich was the second largest town after
London, and was a major textile centre. The causes of the rebellion
are symptomatic of the confused nature of lower order discontent
against the economic changes. The rising was triggered by unrest over
enclosures. East Anglia had a large number of independent small
farmers, who were being adversely affected by gentry and yeomen
enclosing fields and commons. At the same time, the collapse of
textile exports had thrown large numbers of clothworkers in Norwich
and the surrounding countryside out of work. In June there were riots
at the neighbouring market towns of Attleborough and Wymondham,
and some new fences that had been put up by Sir John Flowerdew

were pulled down. Flowerdew was a lawyer who had bought up church property in the area. This made him unpopular with the locals, who resented him as an outsider. Furthermore, he was in dispute with the townspeople of Wymondham over the local abbey, which he had bought and was pulling down. The townspeople had bought the abbey church for use by the parish, and were incensed when Flowerdew began to strip the lead from the roof. Flowerdew was also in dispute with Robert Kett, a local yeoman, over land. Kett himself had enclosed much of the common at Wymondham, and Flowerdew tried to turn the rioters against him. Kett, in the tradition of good neighbourliness, turned the tables by offering to act as spokesman for the rioters. He quickly gathered an army of 16,000 men, and in July was able to capture Norwich. Like the other popular uprisings (see page 86), the rebellion was eventually crushed, and Kett was hanged for sedition.

Articles of the Norfolk Rebels, 1549

1 We pray your grace that where it is enacted for enclosing [legislation against enclosure] that it be not hurtful to such as enclosed ... and that henceforth no man shall enclose any more.
   We pray that Redeground [grassland] and meadow grounds may be
5 at such price as they were in the first year of King Henry the VII.
   We pray that all freeholders and copyholders may take the profits of all commons, and there to common, and the lords not to common nor take profits from the same.
   We pray that copyhold land that is not reasonably rented may go as
10 it did in the first year of King Henry VII and that at the death of a tenant or of a sale of the same lands to be charged with an easy fine as a capon [a light down payment such as a chicken] or a reasonable sum of money for a remembrance [token].
   We pray that all bond men [serfs] may be free for God made all free
15 with his precious blood shedding.
   We pray that rivers may be free and open to all men for fishing and passage.

There were sixteen more articles, covering a range of topics, such as sea fishing, dovecots, rabbits, bullocks, and priests, who were also seen by the rebels as exploiting the economic situation. The six articles given above are quite typical of the remainder. The first is interesting because, apart from local incidents such as at Wymondham and Attleborough, there had been relatively few enclosures in Norfolk during the previous 50 years. Similarly, the request that serfs should be made free seems to be going back to past struggles, because there is no evidence that there were any unfree tenants in sixteenth-century Norfolk. The major demands were for commons to be kept open and free for the husbandmen to graze their livestock, and that rents should not be increased excessively. Just as the West Country rebels seemed to wish for religion to be returned to the good old days of Henry VIII, the Norfolk insurgents appeared to yearn for the favourable economic conditions that existed under Henry VII. This does seem to support the notion that the major cause of the popular unrest in 1549 was the harsh economic conditions that prevailed in that year.

7 Assessment

At all levels mid-Tudor society appears to have been more in a process of fairly stable evolution than in a state of crisis and conflict. There was considerable underlying continuity, although significant differences had emerged. Society appears to have reached a point where the changes taking place over the previous two centuries had been consolidated. English society was about to enter the next phase of its development, which was to bring even greater structural change. At this point any stresses appear to have come from potential crises in the economy, rather than a crisis in society.

Working on Chapter 5

In order really to understand the political and religious changes taking place it is important that you know something about mid-Tudor society at all levels. Although political decisions were made by the elites, popular reaction and lower order uprisings were important issues, especially in 1549. This chapter examines the evolution of English society from the end of the Middle Ages, and assesses whether this process had created a mid-Tudor social crisis. You should note down the various general social theories and decide whether they and social models are useful ways of studying social changes. Then you need to note how the Tudors saw their own society in 1522 and in the middle of the century. Finally, your notes should set out the case for and against a mid-Tudor social crisis. When doing this, it is important that you make your own judgement on the validity of the arguments on both sides. The questions posed in the issues boxes will help to structure your notes.

Answering structured and essay questions on Chapter 5

This section will examine how to answer 'significance' type of questions.

Examiners often set questions suggesting that a certain factor was the most signicant or most important cause of a certain event, or they might ask how significant one event was in causing another. Such questions are designed to test your ability to identify important issues and argue a convincing case to support your judgement. Remember

Summary Diagram
A Crisis in Society?

(a) The Feudal Social Hierarchy c. 1350

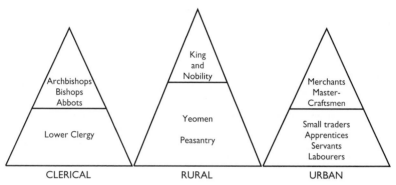

Summary Diagram
A Crisis in Society?

(b) The Early Tudor Social Hierarchy c. 1550

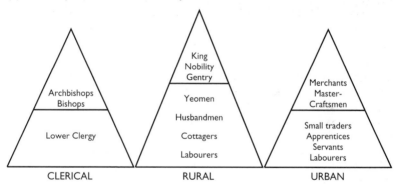

that in many cases the examiner is expecting you to argue against the proposal in the question, or at least to show that other events or issues were just important. A good approach to this type of question is to divide the main body of your answer into two parts. You should start by assessing why the proposed 'most significant', or 'how significant' event or issue could be considered highly important. Then in the second part you should suggest (supported by evidence) a number of alternatives which you consider to be more, or at least, equally significant. Your conclusion should decide what was the most significant cause or result, or how significant an event or issue was in relation to other things that were happening.

Test your knowledge of mid-Tudor society by answering the following questions:

1a) What were the most important changes to the structure of the lower orders that took place between 1350 and 1550? *(20 marks)*
  b) Do you agree that the most significant change in elite Tudor society was the 'rise of the gentry'? *(20 marks)*
2. How significant was religious change in altering the structure of mid-Tudor society?
3. Was 'enclosure' the most significant cause of unrest among the lower orders in 1549?

Source-based questions on Chapter 5

The following questions will test your insight into mid-Tudor society.

1. Shellingford in 1522
Study the extract from the muster certificate for Shellingford, which includes all the details about individuals (page 115). Answer the following questions:

a) How accurate was it likely to be? *(2 marks)*
b) Assuming that the average family numbered 4.5, how many people lived in the village? *(2 marks)*
c) Assuming that movable property to the value of four pounds and above indicates a self-sufficient family, how many people in the village would have depended on wages for part of their income? Explain your answer. *(4 marks)*

2. The Structure of Society in 1565
Read the extract from Sir Thomas Smith's *The Commonwealth of England* given on page 119. Answer the following questions:

a) Explain the meaning of 'the port, charge and countenance of a gentleman' (lines 11-12). *(3 marks)*
b) What are the four classes of society that Smith identifies? (4 marks)
c) To which class does Smith probably belong? Explain your answer. *(4 marks)*
d) How reliable is this extract as evidence of the structure of mid-Tudor society? *(3 marks)*

3. The Norfolk Rebels of 1549
Read the extract from the articles of the Norfolk rebels, given on page 125, and answer the following questions:

a) What is meant by (i) 'commons' (line 7) and (ii) 'copyhold land' (line 9)? *(2 marks)*
b) What evidence does the extract provide to support the view that 'the rebels were primarily reacting against a worsening economic situation'? *(6 marks)*
c) Using your own knowledge, explain why the rebels were unsuccessful in obtaining redress for their grievances? *(4 marks)*

6 A Crisis in the Economy?

POINTS TO CONSIDER

This chapter examines the extent to which the English economy had developed by 1558. In pre-industrial societies changes in population levels had a huge impact on the economy. You should note carefully what effect population levels were having on the mid-Tudor economy. Next you need to consider how and why the agricultural sector had become more efficient by the 1550s. Then you should assess why the industrial sector was unable to find employment for surplus labour. The next step is to decide to what extent the causes of the mid-century trade recession were more political than economic. Finally, you should list the reasons why is it no longer thought that there was a mid-Tudor economic crisis.

KEY DATES

1349	Black Death and beginning of recurrent bubonic plague epidemics
1470s	End of population decrease and deflation and beginning of population increase and inflation
1500	Prices started to rise faster than wages
1537-48	Series of good harvests
1549	Poor harvest and widespread popular discontent
1552	Plague and sweating sickness checked population rise
1552-53	Trade embargoes marked beginning of decline of Antwerp and beginning of commercial slump
1554-56	Severe harvest failures
1556-58	Influenza epidemics caused fall in population
1558	Loss of Calais

1 Approaches and Problems of Interpretation

> **KEY ISSUES** Why have the approaches to, and interpretation of, the early Tudor economy changed in recent years? In what ways do problems of evidence make it difficult to analyse the pre-industrial economy?

Although the idea of a general mid-Tudor crisis is no longer fashionable, it is still thought that there might have been a crisis in the economy. To appreciate why the mid-Tudor economy is still considered to be very fragile it is necessary to understand how economic historians study pre-industrial economies.

a) General Theories and Models

During the post-war debate (see page 4) economic historians, like the social scientists, were producing general theories and models to explain the 'transition from feudalism to capitalism'. Although considerble similaries were seen to exist between economic and social change, the economists concentrated on trying to explain the coming of the Industrial Revolution in Britain. They used the idea of the expansion of capitalism to explain why Britain had emerged as the first industrialised nation by the end of the eighteenth century. The development of capitalism in Tudor England was seen as the first stage of a process leading almost inevitably to the Industrial Revolution. A revolution in agriculture led to commercial expansion which culminated in the Industrial Revolution. This was explained in terms of 'proto-industrialisation'. The emergence of a rural cottage industry in Tudor England (proto-industrialisation) was considered to have been the first stage towards industrialisation, eventually leading to the factory system. By the 1980s these ideas, like most general theories, were being abandoned. Research had revealed little evidence of capitalism in Tudor England. Doubts were expressed about there being agricultural revolutions in either the sixteenth or the eighteenth century. It had proved almost impossible to demonstrate that the cottage industry developed into the factory system. The pre-industrial economy is no longer seen in terms of a series of stages of revolutionary growth. Instead, it is considered that there was a process of slow evolutionary change out of which industrial capitalism emerged in the nineteenth century. However, two general theories about pre-indutrial economies proved to be very valid, and they remain a key method of investigating the Tudor economy.

b) Population and Malthusian Crises

i) Malthusian Crises

In 1798 an economist, the Reverend Thomas Malthus, put forward the theory that in pre-industrial economies population growth was limited by the availability of food supply. He suggested that agricultural production normally rose arithmetically (1, 2, 3, 4 etc.), while, if unchecked, population increased geometrically (1, 2, 4, 8 etc.). Wars and disease were two positive checks which could keep populations within the limits of available resources. However, in periods of peace, without some form of contraception, or an increase in food production, population growth would outstrip food supplies. This would create a subsistence crisis resulting in famines, and rising death rates from starvation. Population would fall until it reached a level within the limits of the food supply, and would then start to rise again.

ii) Demographic Determinism

Many post-war economic historians became convinced that population was the key to studying pre-industrial economies. They considered that rising or falling levels of population, by causing inflation or deflation, determined economic growth or decline. It was calculated that between about 1086 and 1280 the English medieval population had risen from about 2 million to about 6 million. It is thought that, by then, population had begun to outstrip food supplies and that there was a Malthusian check with famines causing the population level to fall. Because pre-industrial farming was primitive weather conditions are seen as an important variable in this process. Until about the 1260s Western Europe had enjoyed a long period of good weather known as the 'little optimum', with temperatures 2 degrees Celsius above average. This was followed by a cold spell, known as the 'mini ice age', when temperatures were 2 degrees Celsius below average, which lasted until the eighteenth century. The beginning of the 'mini ice age', by increasing the number of harvest failures, is thought to have added to the problems of the late medieval economy. Even so, the population had begun to recover by the 1340s, when, in 1349, England was devastated by the Black Death. The population fell by a third, and further recurrent outbreaks of bubonic plague reduced the population to about 1.5 million by the 1460s. This produced a deflationary period of low rents, low prices and high wages, to the detriment of the elites and the benefit of the lower orders. By 1500 the population had begun to recover, beginning an inflationary period which reversed the previous trend, and lasted until the 1650s

Such processes are clearly highly relevant to the question of a possible mid-Tudor economic crisis. The middle decades of the sixteenth century experienced unemployment, harvest failures and sharply rising food prices, until epidemics eventually halted the rise in population. It has been suggested that this amounted to a Malthusian crisis, but by no means all economists are convinced that the problems were so acute.

c) Measurement of Pre-industrial Economic Growth

Another orthodox approach is to study the occupational distribution of the population to detect signs of economic growth. This is achieved by calculating how the movement of people altered the employment balance within the economy. By measuring the shifts in the number of people employed in different occupations between the various economic sectors, it can be calculated whether an economy was backward or advanced. Economies in which most people were employed in agriculture, forestry or fishing are considered to have been the most primitive. This was still the case in England in 1500. The bulk of the population were producing enough to feed their own families, along with a surplus which was paid as rents, tithes and taxes to support the elites, the clergy and the government bureaucracy. This generally left little or nothing to be spent on manufactured and other consumer goods. Consequently, towns, manufacturing and commerce remained on a small scale. Once a distinct movement of human resources out of these areas into a more economically advanced sector (such as manufacturing or commerce) can be discerned, then the economy is considered to have been expanding. So, if by the middle of the sixteenth century there was a movement of people out of agriculture into industry, the English economy could be considered to be growing. In theory this sounds easy, but, of course, in practice it is much less simple.

The difficulty is that there are other considerations to be taken into account. If people were moving out of agriculture then they were becoming less self-sufficient, and more dependent upon the food markets. This meant that agriculture had to be more efficient to produce enough food to support the increasing number of wage-earners. At the same time sixteenth-century industry mainly used raw materials, such as wool, wood and leather, produced by agriculture. Consequently, if industry was to expand, more raw materials had to be produced. However, the danger was that agriculture might prove to be unable to produce either enough food or sufficient raw materials. If this were the case there would be food shortages, a slump in industry and economic decline. The question of whether or not there was a mid-century economic crisis hinges very much on this issue.

d) Variations in Interpretation

Within these broad approaches there are a variety of explanations of economic advance or decline. Developments in agriculture, industry, towns, internal trade or overseas commerce are put forward as of paramount importance in the achievement of economic growth.

i) Agriculture
It is difficult to decide which sector was having the greatest impact on the state of the economy in the middle of the sixteenth century. As the country was still overwhelmingly rural, changes in agriculture must be seen as of prime importance. A strong case has been made for there having been an agricultural revolution in the sixteenth century, based upon commercialisation and new techniques. Evolutionists reject this idea on the basis that the use of fresh skills was on too small a scale and too localised to be revolutionary, although they do agree that there was greater commercial input. Commercialisation can be interpreted as either resulting from the emergence of the gentry and the yeomen, or being brought about by the entrepreneurial influence of merchants buying country estates.

Equally, it can be argued that the agricultural expansion of the early sixteenth century was merely the natural result of population growth and inflation.

ii) Industry

The situation in the industrial sector is just as vexed. Here, too, it has been suggested that there was a revolution, based in this instance on the coal industry, which caused a decisive shift towards capitalistically intensive, heavy production. Although there is no support among modern historians for the idea of a sixteenth-century industrial revolution, it is agreed that industry was becoming more capital intensive. What is in dispute is the form of commercial development that was taking place. Although the idea of 'proto-industrialisation' is no longer accepted, it is agreed that the rural cottage industry was a highly important growth area. However, other historians still maintain that the development of capital intensive fixed plant, such as mills and furnaces, was more significant. Even the question of measuring the movement of the workforce into more economically advanced sectors is regarded as very difficult. Any shifts depend upon such variables as the mobility of labour, and the availability of capital and technology. Equally necessary was the existence of effective transport and communications to promote urban growth and to create an internal market. Moreover, such conditions are seen as being dependent on government attitudes. The State, as the largest investor in the economy, is regarded as a major promoter of economic growth. However, State intervention, with legislation against enclosures and vagrancy, can be seen as inhibiting commercialisation and the movement of labour.

iii) Overseas Commerce

Within the wider context of western Europe and the development of world trade, England was a backward offshore island in the first half of the sixteenth century. The whole of the western European economy is seen as being labour intensive, with low levels of production and little fixed capital. Demand is considered to have been inelastic in that it could only be increased by creating new markets outside Europe rather than by expanding trade within the existing home market. Compared with the continent, the English economy is considered to have been deficient in almost every respect. In commercial terms, England, apart from the sale of semi-finished cloth, was an exporter of raw materials and an importer of manufactured and luxury goods. Moreover, it was not until after the 1560s that England is seen as playing any significant part in the development of the world trade routes pioneered by Spain and Portugal. In terms of agriculture, industry and commerce, the Netherlands is regarded as being much more advanced than England. German mining techniques and heavy industry, and the textile industries in France, Italy and Spain are considered far superior in quality and technology to their English counterparts. However, the first half of the sixteenth century is thought by many economic historians to have been a time when England began to catch up with the continent. For this reason the middle of the century can be seen as an important watershed – a turning point – in economic terms. The difficulties and restructuring of the first part of the century are considered to have produced conditions suitable for a renewal of modest economic growth. However, what needs to be estimated is whether the mid-century English economy experienced a crisis in reaching this position and, if so, what was the nature and extent of the problem.

e) Difficulties Caused by the Lack of Reliable Data

Any analysis of the economy requires reliable data upon which to base statistics. Over the centuries historical records have been lost, destroyed by floods and fires and eaten by rats and mice, so that the surviving evidence is very patchy and incomplete. In any case, there was no systematic record-keeping by the central or local authorities. The evidence that does exist is fragmentary, unreliable and often unsuitable for quantification. This problem extends to all parts of the economy, but is particularly acute when comes to compiling population statistics. Given that population levels now are seen as prime indicators of economic performance, this is a major problem. Before the census of 1801 the authorities had compiled no national population records, although the Church and some towns had conducted a few local censuses. The muster certificates for 1522 (see page 114), provide a useful basis for calculating early Tudor population levels, but they have not survived for many parts of the country. At the same time, as is the case with many Tudor documents, they mainly listed male heads of households and men of military age This means that it is necessary to calculate the number of women and children and other dependants who made up the normal household. It is generally accepted that a reasonable estimate of population can be obtained by multiplying the listed heads of household by 4.5. However, the problem of population figures has to some extent been overcome by using parish registers of births, marriages and deaths, which began to be kept in some areas from 1538. The Cambridge Group of demographers used these registers to project population figures back from the known data in the nineteenth century to the sixteenth century by tracing families listed in the registers. The results of this family reconstruction was published in 1981 – E.A. Wrigley and R.S. Schofield, *The Population History of England 1541-1871: A Reconstruction* – and is accepted as the best possible estimate of early modern population figures even by its critics. Unfortunately the deficiencies in the surviving data for the remainder of the economy cannot be so satisfactorily resolved. The inaccuracy of many of the births and deaths registers makes it difficult to calculate fertility and mortality rates. The cause of death was rarely recorded in burial registers, which, along with the lack of medical knowledge in Tudor England, makes it very difficult to calculate the extent and nature of epidemics. Wage levels and prices were set by the local magistrates and varied widely across the country. This makes it difficult to calculate living standards, or compare the fortunes of a family living in Kent with one from Yorkshire. The buying and selling of goods in towns and local markets went virtually unrecorded. Records of imports and exports are very patchy and unsystematic, and even the large ports, such as London or Bristol, often used different systems of book keeping. Weights and measures varied widely and differed between commodities – a tun of flour measured 1,800 pounds, while a tun of sugar or butter weighed 2,240 pounds. The fragmentary nature and unreliability of Tudor records means that any statistics are, at the best, only tentative estimates.

2 Population, Inflation and the Standard of Living

> **KEY ISSUES** What were the main influences on the pattern of demographic recovery and growth between 1500 and 1558? Were population levels beginning to outstrip resources by 1549? What was the main cause of rising inflation? In what ways had inflation influenced living standards? Why were economic problems probably the basic cause of popular discontent in 1549?

a) Demographic Recovery and Growth

There is considerable debate over the changing rates of population growth and its effects during the sixteenth century, particularly in the period between 1500 and 1558.

i) Population Recovery, 1470-1522

After the sharp demographic decline following the Black Death and the subsequent plague cycle (see page 14), population levels are considered to have ceased to fall by about 1470. This was followed by a slow recovery from about 1.5 million in 1470 to some 2.3 million by the 1520s. There is broad agreement about this pattern of demographic decline and recovery, but not about the causes for the revival. There is little dispute that the bubonic plague, carried by the fleas of the black rat, was the cause of the initial catastrophic population losses. What is less clear is what caused the recovery after 1470. Bubonic plague was still endemic, along with a number of other diseases such as influenza, cholera, malaria and typhus. This makes it difficult to maintain that a fall in the rate of mortality was a major reason for a re-growth in population. However, some historians consider that people were beginning to build up immunity to some forms of disease. Others suggest that vulnerability to epidemics varied and changed between age groups. It is claimed that the reason for recovery in population levels could have been that young adults were becoming less susceptible to diseases. If more young women survived, increased numbers of children were likely to be born, which would account for a rise in population. Alternatively it is claimed that there was a drop in infant mortality, which similarly would have led to a rise in the demographic levels.

ii) Population Growth, 1522-50

The situation between 1522 and 1550 is equally uncertain. It is estimated that the population was growing at approximately one per cent per year until 1550, when it possibly just exceeded 3 million. However, the rate of expansion was not even. It is suggested that there was only a very slow improvement until 1540, followed by rapid growth over the next decade, and that by 1558 population levels were falling back again. Once again there is no single explanation for this pattern of events. It is suggested that a major factor was the presence of endemic disease. From the end of the fifteenth century a new virus had joined the killer diseases that were already present. The 'English sweat', a fever which spread more quickly than the plague, was particularly virulent between 1485 and 1528, and could kill within 24 hours. It struck particularly at young adults, and it is thought that this, by reducing the birthrate, slowed the rate of population increase up to 1540. Moreover there were four serious outbreaks of plague between 1500 and 1528, and another in the late 1530s, to which adolescents were especially vulnerable. However, it is felt that the comparative absence of epidemics between 1528 and 1550 might well account for the sharp demographic increase in the 1540s. Again, it is suggested that a fall in infant mortality might have been a major cause for more children surviving into adulthood.

iii) Checks to Population Growth, 1551-58

The substantial check to population increase in the 1550s is easier to explain. In 1551 and 1552 there were fresh outbreaks of plague and sweating sickness. Even more serious was the influenza epidemic which ravaged the whole country between 1556 and 1558. It is estimated that it had a mortality rate of at least six per cent, and that the population might have been reduced to under 3 million. To add to the difficulties of obtaining a clear picture, there were considerable local variations in population densities, the rate of increase or decline, and in the incidence of disease. In broad terms the south-eastern section of England was more heavily populated than the north-west because of the different farming regions (see page 142). Towns, particularly London, which had high concentrations of people, were especially susceptible to epidemics, but the rate of recovery was normally rapid. East Anglia was the most highly populated area, while the north of England had the least number of people per square mile. In sparsely settled areas epidemics were less likely, but the rate of recovery from any population losses was slower.

iv) Variations in Recovery and Growth

There is ample evidence from empty houses and abandoned plots of land in both towns and villages that the population during the first half of the sixteenth century had not recovered from earlier losses. In north Berkshire the village of Hinton, even by 1573, had not recovered the level of population that it had in 1381. In contrast, a survey of the nearby market town of Wantage in the 1550s estimated that the town's population was 1,000; a figure confirmed by calculations from the parish registers. This compares with a population of 600 in 1522 – a rise of 66 per cent over 30 years, and twice the estimated national average. The level of increase in the neighbouring villages was lower, and in some cases there was an actual decrease. It is very difficult to pinpoint the causes of such discrepancies in the countryside, and between villages within a few miles of each other. Much of the similarly varied demographic fortunes of towns in early Tudor England can be attributed to the random outbreak of disease. The three largest towns after London – Norwich, Bristol and York – all suffered severe epidemics in the middle of the century. Indeed, it is calculated that the population of Norwich remained stationary between 1522 and 1558, which is in marked contrast to the growth of London and some other towns.

b) A Malthusian Crisis by 1549?

Although the evidence for rising population levels is complicated, and often contradictory, it has been suggested that there may have been overpopulation by 1549, leading to a subsistence, or Malthusian crisis. The effect of the 'mini ice age' (see page 131) was to introduce cooler and wetter weather, which is considered to have shortened the growing season. These conditions persisted throughout the sixteenth century, with alternating spells of good and bad weather. The result was that there were sequences of good, poor and very poor harvests. There were bad harvests from 1527 to 1529, 1549 to 1551 and 1554 to 1556, although only the exceptionally bad harvests of 1555 and 1556 were poor enough to produce an actual dearth, or famine, on a wide scale. However, there were problems at a local level, such as the chronic food shortages in Coventry during the 1520s and possibly at Norwich in 1532. There were good harvests from 1537 to 1542, and 1546 to 1548. The poor harvests in the 1520s and 1550s coincided with epidemics and probably increased the mortality rate, while the plague epidemic of the late 1530s occurred during a run of good harvests and possibly had less effect. Epidemics and runs of good or bad harvests accentuated the underlying demographic trend. The almost unbroken run of good harvests during the 1540s would have lowered grain prices, and so have raised living standards for the mass of the population. In turn, this may have encouraged earlier marriage, and so intensified the upward spiral in population levels. Consequently, the poor harvest of 1549 may have created a subsistence crisis, which was an underlying cause of the widespread popular unrest in that year.

On the weight of the existing evidence it is no longer considered likely that there was a Malthusian crisis in 1549. Population growth was not checked in 1549 and continued to rise until the influenza epidemics of the 1550s. Even at its height in 1550, the population level was only about half that which had been supported early in the fourteenth century. Consequently, even with enclosure and increased regional specialisation, (see page 142) there should have been ample farmland to support the population. Moreover, as there had previously been a long run of good harvests, a very adequate supply of stored grain should have remained even in the towns. It is suggested that lower order hostility towards enclosure in Norfolk and elsewhere was not because it created local grain shortages, but because husbandmen felt that gentry competition was undermining their own agricultural specialisation (see page 145). In any case, the mid-century harvest failures appear to have been caused by abnormally wet summers rather than over-cropping. The harvest failures in the mid-1550s were much more severe, but by then population levels had fallen back because of high mortality rates during the epidemics. It is generally thought that causes other than food shortages must be found to explain the widespread lower order discontent in 1549. Even so, the sharp increase in population during the 1540s helps to explain the government's anxieties over enclosures, vagrancy and the need to maintain the acreage of arable land.

c) Inflation

i) Causes

Inflation, which is estimated to have been 400 per cent over the whole of the century, is seen as another major contributor to the economic pressures that existed by the middle of the century. In the past it was thought that the large amount of silver imported by Spain into western Europe from South America was the major cause of inflation in the sixteenth century. This view is no longer widely held, and it is thought that South American silver had little effect on English inflation until the end of the century. It is widely agreed that a rising population, which increased demand, was the underlying cause of inflation. However, this alone does not explain the pattern of inflation during the first half of the century. The 'price scissors', the point when prices and rents overtook wages, is seen as occurring soon after

1500. Prices and rents continued to rise until after 1550, but until 1540 the actual rise in population was slow. Even by the 1530s grain and meat prices were increasing quite rapidly in town markets, and may have doubled between 1510 and 1530. Historians attribute this trend in part to the poor harvests of the 1520s, but prices showed no sign of falling even by the late 1520s after a run of good harvests. The reason for this, it is thought, was that commercial farmers were still concentrating on pasture for wool production. This, and enclosure, are seen to be the underlying causes for the upward spiral of rents. By the 1540s population pressure added to the upward movement of inflation.

Other forces were at work to create high inflation by 1550. Debasements of the coinage, which began in 1526, became very frequent in the 1540s, when the government was desperately trying to raise money to finance the wars against France and Scotland (see page 37). By increasing the amount of money in circulation while devaluing the coinage, debasement caused very rapid inflation of prices. At the same time the Reformation may well have contributed to this process. Gold and silver ornaments, seized from the monasteries, chantries and churches, were melted down and turned into coins, so adding to the volume of debased coinage in circulation. By 1550 the rate of inflation may have reached 200 per cent over the first half of the century, and the very high levels of inflation reached by 1549 may well have contributed to the widespread popular discontent. By 1553 epidemics had eased population pressure and so slowed the rate of inflation. At the same time, government reforms of the currency reduced the amount of coinage in circulation. The effect was to reduce the rate of inflation still further, which might help to explain the lack of popular unrest during the bad harvests of the mid-1550s.

ii) Rents and Wages

The levels of rents and wages are seen as another possible contributor to popular unrest, because they too had a direct effect on the standard of living. With relatively sluggish population growth up to 1540, it might be expected that rents and wages would remain comparatively stable. As far as wages were concerned this is exactly what happened. In the south of England the wages for rural workers remained at 4d. a day and for building workers at 6d. a day until the 1550s. This meant that the level of wages obtained in the fifteenth century when population was very low was maintained in spite of the increase in population. However, because of the considerable increase in inflation, the standard of living of all wage-earners is considered to have fallen. The evidence of the level of rents is less conclusive. In some areas, especially around London, rents were certainly going up by the 1530s, and may even have more than doubled from 6d. per acre to 13d. per acre. In other areas, away from south-eastern England, they appear to have remained static, and in some places may even have fallen slightly. The pressure was heaviest on pasture land because of the demand for wool and other animal products. Enclosed land commanded higher rents, and may have affected levels of rent in the surrounding district.

Although the evidence is not conclusive, it is felt that resentment over the level of rents and wages may have added to popular discontent, especially in the southern half of the country. The problem is that there is no clear distinction between smallholders and labourers. Although it is estimated that over 40 per cent of the population were wage-earners – 10 per cent working in industry – only a minority were full-time employees. Many smallholders supplemented their incomes by wages, and most workers in cottage and other industries had their own smallholdings. A large number of town labourers spent part of the year working in the countryside, especially at harvest time. This makes it very difficult to select any one particular cause for economic discontent among the lower orders, and large-scale uprisings may have been caused by groups with different grievances coming together for mutual support.

iii) The Standard of Living

In spite of the conflicting evidence there are some clear links between living standards and popular discontent in the middle of the century. Even if the standard of living of the mass of the population had not fallen as dramatically as it was once assumed, it had certainly not improved. Clearly the rebels in Norfolk felt that their economic position had declined since the end of the fifteenth century, and blamed it largely on rising rents (see page 125). The groups which had generally gained from increased rents and prices were the elites, the yeomen, merchants, industrialists, and some husbandmen. Consequently part of the problem in 1549 might have been the general economic resentment of those who felt they were the losers, against those groups which they felt were gaining. However, it must be remembered that it is too simple to make such a clear-cut distinction. Within each grouping there were both winners and losers. Unrest in 1549 was very localised, and a riot or rebellion might have been sparked off by one individual who thought that his neighbour had cheated him or was becoming unduly prosperous.

iv) Assessment of the Year 1549

Another way of looking at 1549 is to see it as a particularly bad year, which experienced the conjunction of a number of unrelated problems rather than any one specific difficulty. The bad harvest after a run of good seasons, which pushed up grain prices, would obviously have caused discontent. However, this was not the sole cause, because there was already unrest in 1548 when the harvest was good. A combination of a weak government, mismanaged policies, religious change and reverses in the war had produced an atmosphere of disquiet by 1549. The additional economic problems of high inflation and population pressure may well have turned disquiet into discontent and open rebellion.

3 Agriculture

> **KEY ISSUES** How had agricultural methods of production changed since the late Middle Ages? Although new crops and techniques were being used, had these increased the supply of basic foodstuffs by the 1550s? Why is it no longer thought that there was a Malthusian crisis in 1549?

As the largest sector in the mid-sixteenth-century English economy, and the employer of the bulk of the population, agriculture had a considerable influence on the economy. However, as agricultural development is now seen as a very slow evolutionary process, it is difficult to pinpoint precisely what stage it had reached by the mid-century.

a) Changes in Land Usage

Apart from importing food from abroad, pre-industrial farmers had two basic ways in which to increase output to feed rising populations. The easiest method was simply to clear and cultivate more land. The more difficult option was to produce a greater quantity of food from the same amount of land. During the medieval population expansion the problem had been met by clearing more land. However, this had eventually meant cultivating increasingly marginal land unsuited to arable farming. In the end, this, and the climatic down-turn, had resulted in poorer yields and harvest failures. The result was a subsistence crisis and the breakdown of the late medieval economy.

By the fifteenth century there was no problem in feeding the drastically reduced population. This enabled a withdrawal from the poorer land, which had been made even more marginal by the change to cooler and wetter weather conditions. Whole areas, such as the Brecklands in Norfolk and Dartmoor in the West Country, were virtually abandoned. In every county many villages on the poorer or wetter soils were deserted, and were never reoccupied. This meant that large tracts of previously cultivated land reverted to grassland and pasture, which enabled more cattle and sheep to be kept. The remaining areas of arable were on the richer soils, or, at least, those soils which would support cultivation with the extra quantity of manure available. This means that English agriculture should have been able to move on to the more advanced stage of of producing sufficient food from a smaller acreage of arable land. The evidence suggests that without the constant pressure to produce cereals, farming began to become more specialised. This raises the question as to why England in 1550, with a population of only just over 3 million, appears to have been barely able to feed this comparatively small number of people.

b) Changing Methods

i) Land Usage

Part of the answer to this question lies in the nature of the changes in agriculture taking place after the collapse of the late-medieval economy. One of the problems with medieval farming was that it had been largely dominated by 'peasant production methods'. A peasant smallholder had had to produce a range of foodstuffs from the land in order to meet all the needs of his family. This form of production took no account of the wide variety of soil types or their suitability for general farming. Therefore, peasant cultivation was often inefficient and wasteful. However, even during the Middle Ages, peasants had had to adapt their farming techniques to meet the differing conditions imposed by moorlands, fens or forest. After 1350 the reduction in the number of smallholdings meant that gentry, yeomen and husbandmen could begin to specialise within the broader agricultural zones. The two major zones are delineated by a line running from Newcastle in the north-east to Exmouth in the south-west. The upland area west and north of this line has thinner soils with a cooler, wetter climate, making it more suitable for pastoral farming. The lowland area to the south and east of the line has richer soils with a warmer and drier climate better suited to arable farming. Within these zones specialisations began to develop, such as dairy farming in Wiltshire or cereal production in East Anglia.

ii) New Crops and Techniques

This growing agricultural variety makes it difficult to decide how far farming had progressed by the middle of the sixteenth century. During the sixteenth century new techniques, crops and methods of field rotation were introduced. A number of new crops, such as clover and lucerne, were being grown to improve fodder for animal feed. Industrial crops such as saffron, woad and rapeseed were being grown to produce dyes and oils for textile manufacture. At the same time it is suggested that improvements were being made to the techniques of breeding cattle and sheep.

iii) Enclosure

A vital part of this process of improvement was considered to be the spread of enclosure from about 1450 onwards. This, it is thought, enabled the growth of more efficient median-sized farms, which had flexible field systems. These new layouts began to replace the old three-field system, where an individual farmer's land was scattered in small plots across the open fields. At the same time much of the common land was enclosed and brought under more intensive cultivation. It was these developments that are considered to have enabled the introduction of greater specialisation and new techniques. 'Up and down husbandry' was a system under which land was used alternatingly over a number of years as arable and then for pasture. This technique is seen to have prevented soil exhaustion, and to have maintained a better balance between arable and grazing land. Further improvements were made to grazing land by the use of floating water meadows – riverside pastures which were flooded every year with the aid of sluices so that the river silt would enhance the quality of the grass.

iv) An Agriculture Revolution?

It was suggested by E. Kerridge in *The Agricultural Revolution*, 1961, that these advances revolutionised Tudor agriculture. This idea has now largely fallen out of favour, and has been replaced by the notion of slower, more evolutionary development. There is wide agreement that all these improvements were taking place at some time, and in some places, during the sixteenth century. However, evolutionists argue very strongly that a few people using some new techniques does not make a revolution. They maintain that any changes were extremely localised, and were only adopted very slowly between 1500 and 1750. While these improvements certainly led to greater per acre, and per capita, output by the 1650s, it is impossible to tell whether this had led to any increase in production by the 1550s. It is agreed that three things were most likely to lead to greater farming output. These were, the more efficient commercial farms being created by the gentry and yeomen, the greater acreage of good land brought under cultivation through enclosure, and the introduction of new crops and techniques. However, enclosure and commercialisation were the very things being blamed by the government and its critics for the economic problems in the middle of the sixteenth century.

c) Assessment of Mid-Tudor Agriculture

The reason for this is that, although changes were taking place in agriculture, they had not had any appreciable improvement to the levels of cereal production by the mid-century. Indeed, it is considered that enclosure was possibly the cause of this problem. In the first half of the sixteenth century, the gentry and yeomen, who were mainly responsible for enclosure, were clearly looking for the most profitable crops to gain a good return on their investment. During periods of high population grain prices rose, and so enclosed fields, which were ideal for growing cereals, would be used for this purpose. It is thought that in response to a rising population, increasing numbers of commercial farmers converted to cereals. By the seventeenth century production was so efficient that grain prices actually fell in spite of a continued rise in population. However, during the first half of the sixteenth century population increase was almost imperceptible until after 1540. For this reason farmers were slow to shift to cereals, preferring to use enclosed land as sheep-runs, so as to profit from high wool prices. Consequently, because of the spurt in population in the 1540s, there may have been localised pressure on grain supplies by 1549.

Specialisation may well have added to this problem by increasing the number of agricultural regions. Many such areas were created by yeomen and husbandmen responding to local demands and adapting to the types of soil on which they farmed. A good example of this is Wiltshire, where the heavy soils were particularly suited to cattle-raising, and dairy farming became a speciality. Small dairy herds were attractive to husbandmen because they could be managed with family labour, and brought in a regular income from milk, butter and cheese. Larger scale cattle-rearing and fattening was usually outside the scope of the husbandmen because it required more capital investment. Whatever type of specialism was adopted, new agricultural regions created problems for grain supplies during the first part of the sixteenth century. Not only did they lower the overall national cereal output, but each specialist region became increasingly dependent upon surrounding areas for grain and other farm products. For a regional farming structure to work efficiently a good infrastructure of roads and navigable rivers was needed so that produce could be moved rapidly from one part of the country to another. The government and local authorities were aware of the problem. Attempts were made to improve river navigation, particularly on the Thames, and local landowners worked with the town authorities to improve roads. However, it is considered that little real progress was made until after the 1560s.

i) A Contemporary View of the Situation

Such a view is supported by Sir Thomas Smith in another of his books, *A Discourse on the Commonweal of this Realm of England* (see page 119). This takes the form of a dialogue between a doctor, representing the academic view, discussing the state of the economy with various members of society such as a knight, a merchant and a husbandman. After suggesting that the debasing of the coinage had doubled prices in his lifetime, the doctor goes on to discuss the cost and shortage of grain. He suggests that the best way to get more grain was either to make it as expensive as wool, or to reduce the price of wool.

1   Doctor: Marry the first way is to make that wool be of as base a price [to] the breeder thereof as corn is; and that shall be, if you make alike restraints of wools, for passing over the sea unwrought, [unfinished]

as ye make corn. [On the other hand] Would you make corn dearer
5 than it is? Have you dearth enough else without that?
Husbandman: I thank you with all my heart; for you have spoken in the
matter more [better] than I could do myself ... We felt the harm, but
we wist not what was the cause thereof; many of us saw, 12 years ago,
that our profits was small by the plough; and therefore divers [various]
10 of my neighbours that had in times past, some two, some three, some
four ploughs of their own, have laid [them] down ... and turned either
part or all their arable ground into pasture, and thereby have waxed
very rich men. And every day some of us encloseth a plot of his ground
to pasture; and were it not that our ground lieth in the common fields,
15 intermingled one with another, I think also our fields had been enclosed,
of a common agreement of all the township [village], long ere this time.
And to say the truth, I, that have enclosed little or nothing of my
ground, could never be able to make up my lord's rent were it not for
a little breed of neat [cattle], sheep, swine, geese, and hens that I do
20 rear upon my ground; whereof, because the price is somewhat round,
I make more clear profit than I do of all my corn; and yet I have a bare
living, by reason that many things do belong to husbandry which now be
exceedingly chargeable over they were in times past.

This view of the economy, confirms that it was not just the gentry and
yeomen who were failing to grow enough grain, but that husbandmen
were equally to blame for any shortfalls. The reason for this appears to
have been the low price of grain in comparison with wool and other
animal products over the previous decades, which had led to the
conversion of arable to pasture. It is interesting to note that
husbandmen appear to have been just as keen to enclose their land as
the larger commercial farmers, and regarded enclosed holdings as
more efficient than the old open fields. Husbandmen clearly were
being adversely affected by increased rents and other agricultural overheads. At the same time they were just as ready to react to market
forces as the larger commercial farmers. This, along with rising rents,
may have been a major cause of popular hostility towards the gentry.
Wool was seen as the quickest way of making a profit from land, but
sheep-runs were a large-scale undertaking and outside the scope of
most husbandmen. It may well have been such commercially-based
rivalry that was an important underlying cause of the disorders in 1549.

4 Rural and Urban Industry

KEY ISSUES Why was heavy industry still relatively backward in the
1550s? How and why had the rural cottage industry become so successful? What were the causes of the conflict between urban and
rural industry?

Developments in industry provide good indicators to show whether or not the mid-Tudor economy was becoming more advanced. The agricultural sector was just about able to feed the population, except in bad harvest years. Less land was under cultivation and this should have meant that, as the population began to rise, surplus labour became available to work in industry. For this to happen more jobs had to be created in both rural and urban industries.

a) Heavy Industry

Heavy industry used to be considered the most dynamic part of the sector. It was suggested by J.U. Nef in *The Rise of the British Coal Industry*, 1932, that there was a Tudor industrial revolution led by rising coal production. This idea was based on the once popular theory that there was a severe timber shortage in Tudor England, and that there was consequently a sharp increase in the use of mineral fuels. The expansion in the industrial use of non-agricultural raw materials, such as coal and other minerals, was seen as being vitally important in the development of early capitalism. Such operations needed expensive equipment on a centralised site and a small, but highly skilled workforce. Mining and metal-working, along with other specialised and capital-intensive undertakings such as dyeing, brewing, glass and paper-making, are regarded as the real signs of a new, capitalistic economy.

i)   Problems in the Coal Industry

These ideas are no longer accepted. It is now thought that any shortages of wood or charcoal were purely local. No sudden rise in demand for coal can be seen until the end of the sixteenth century. A major problem for expansion in heavy industry was the difficulty and cost of transport. Unlike raw materials from agriculture, coal and other minerals were only to be found in certain areas. Consequently, industries associated with these products were very localised because of the cost of carrying heavy materials more than a short distance. It is not considered that any great expansion was possible until real improvements to river navigation and sea transport began in the second half of the sixteenth century. Another difficulty preventing the expansion of heavy industry was that English technology was very backward in comparison with that of the continent. Problems of drainage and ventilation meant that mining operations had to be open cast or through relatively shallow shafts. Coal was mined in south Wales, the Weald of Kent, the Forest of Dean and parts of the Midlands, but on a small scale for local use. The main coal-producing area was Northumberland and Durham, and increasingly large quantities were shipped to London from the end of the fourteenth century. However, this 'sea coal' was used largely for domestic fires and not for industrial purposes.

ii) The Metal Industries

Before the second half of the sixteenth century only small quantities of coal were used in industry. The main reason for this, apart from transport costs, was that heavy industry was localised and only used coal if it was mined nearby. Another important consideration was that coal was unsuitable for iron smelting. Iron ore, like coal, was mined in various places, but mainly in the Weald of Kent and the Forest of Dean, where there was a plentiful supply of timber for making charcoal to smelt the ore. At the end of the fifteenth century, gentry and yeomen ironmasters in the Weald began to use a new type of blast furnace, fuelled by charcoal and powered by water, which had been introduced from the continent. By the 1550s, 26 of these new furnaces were in use in the Weald, making it a major producer of cast iron, which was used particularly for making naval guns and shot. However, pig iron was still the major output. This was converted into bar iron in a finery forge, also fuelled by charcoal and driven by water. The bars of iron were then distributed on pack animals to blacksmiths in the towns and villages for making into tools and other small objects. Apart from the technological advance in iron production, little real progress was made elsewhere before 1560. Tin was mined in Devon and Cornwall mainly for export. Much the same can be said for lead and zinc mining in Shropshire and the Mendips. Although a new blast furnace for smelting lead, which only used half as much fuel, was introduced, the metal-working industries were on a very small scale. It was only after the 1570s that copper, pewter, brass and silver production began to become important. Other specialist, centralised industries such as brick, tile and glass-making, bell-founding and gunpowder manufacture, were still very localised. New, sophisticated processes such as paper-making were only just being introduced.

iii) Assessment of Heavy Industry

By the mid-sixteenth century heavy industry had had little impact on economic growth, and was still at the stage of catching up with continental technology. However, if this sector cannot be said to have made any positive contribution to industrial expansion, neither can it be considered to have added to the economic problems of the mid-century. Apart from a small core of skilled labour, heavy industries only employed casual labour, which, otherwise, would have been under-employed during slack periods in the agricultural year. Consequently, it is thought to be unlikely that this would have had any positive or negative effect on the increasing levels of unemployment by 1550. However, there had been sufficient technical change, innovation, and diversification in this sector to provide a sound base for growth in the second half of the century.

b) Rural Industry

In the thirteenth century many urban textile and leather craftsmen had moved to the countryside to avoid the restrictive practices of the guilds and the high cost of living in towns (see page 16). There they set up new industries to make use of the cheap rural labour force. Crafts such as spinning, weaving, glove-making and basket-making had traditionally been carried out by peasant families in their own homes to supplement their incomes. Craftsmen were able to use this semi-skilled workforce to establish a cottage industry outside the jurisdiction of the town guilds. This was the beginning of the rural textile industry that was to remain dominant until the eighteenth century. Unlike the guilds, which produced small quantities of high quality, expensive goods, rural industries manufactured large amounts of less well made, but much cheaper, products.

i)　The Rural Cloth Industry

The largest branch of cottage industry was textile manufacturing. The significance of this form of cloth production was that it was large-scale and exported increasing quantities of semi-finished textiles to the continent. By the sixteenth century this cottage (or putting-out) industry was organised by clothiers. Generally these were merchants from a nearby town, or local yeomen and prosperous husbandmen. Raw materials such as wool or yarn were purchased by the clothier, who distributed them to his workforce for manufacturing in their cottages using their own tools. This is seen as a significant division of labour because the various stages of manufacture were separated, and only the clothiers sold the completed piece of cloth. It also meant that the clothier had no large outlay to provide buildings or equipment, as was the case in heavy industry. The only high-cost buildings required were the water-driven fulling mills to felt and thicken the woollen cloth by shrinking and rolling it so that the fibres interlocked, and in most cases existing flour mills could be used for this purpose. The capital costs were the purchase of the raw materials and the wages for the workforce. However, until the middle of the sixteenth century it is thought that many of the cottage workforce, particularly the weavers, remained self-employed, and were not entirely dependent on wages. The development of a major exporting industry in England is considered to be a significant economic advance.

The main areas of clothmaking were East Anglia, the West Country, and parts of Yorkshire. In Norfolk fine worsteds were produced, while in the other areas the main products were the highly-prized broadcloths (12 yards by 1.75 yards) and the cheaper, but popular, kerseys (18 yards by 1 yard). Because the English dyeing and finishing trades were technically inferior to those on the continent, the cloth was exported undyed, and semi-finished. This 'white' cloth was finished and dyed on the continent, particularly in the Netherlands, and was then sold by foreign merchants.

ii) Competition between Rural and Urban Industries

Although the rural textile industry is seen as the major contributor to England's economic expansion up to 1550, it did create a number of problems. As the putting-out system was free of guild regulations it was not necessary for those taking part in it to have served an apprenticeship. This caused resentment among the members of the town guilds who saw it as unfair competition. The situation was made worse by the government's failure to enforce regulations in the countryside. Consequently, by the early sixteenth century, apart from textiles, a variety of allied trades, such as leather crafts and stocking knitting, had become firmly established. These also competed with the more expensive products of the urban guilds. From the beginning of the sixteenth century the government repeatedly passed legislation to try to exert greater control over rural industry. In part this was in response to complaints about shoddy workmanship and poor quality goods levelled at the putting-out industry by the towns. At the same time the State was trying to take greater control over the economy in general.

An Act Touching Weavers 1555

1 Foreasmuch as the weavers of this realm have, as well at this present parliament as at divers other times, complained that the rich and wealthy clothiers do many ways oppress them, some by setting up and keeping in their houses divers looms, and keeping and maintain-
5 ing them by journeymen and persons unskilful, to the decay of a great number of artificers which were brought up in the said science of weaving … It is therefore, for remedy of the premises, and for avoiding of a great number of inconveniences which may grow, ordained, established and enacted, by authority of this present
10 parliament, that no person using the feat or mystery of clothmaking, and dwelling out of a city, borough, market town or corporate town, shall … keep, retain or have in his or their house or possession any more or above one woollen loom at one time …

Passed in 1555, the Act Touching Weavers, like its predecessors, proved ineffectual, and it was not until 1563 that the government finally began to exercise some control over rural cloth manufacture. The reason for this success in the 1560s may well have been that by then the textile industry was in the process of a drastic reorganisation. During the 1550s textile exports had slumped, and the production of the 'old draperies' collapsed. Clothmakers had to adjust to demand for a different type of textile, the 'new draperies'. Eventually English manufacturers, with the help of emigrants from the continent, mastered the new techniques, and a renewed export boom began.

> **Enactment of the Common Council of London as to the Age of ending Apprenticeship, 1556**
>
> ı For as much as great poverty, penury, and lack of living hath of late
> years followed ... and one of the chieftest occasions thereof, as it is
> thought ... is by the over hasty marriages and over soon setting up
> of households of and by youth and young folks of the same city ...
> 5 for remedy, stay, and reformation whereof it is ordained ... that no
> manner of persons ...shall be any manner of ways or means made
> free of the said city ... until such time as he and they shall severally
> attain to the age of 24 years.

However, in the 1550s the effect was disastrous. Attempts by the authorities to remedy the situation were generally crude and heavy-handed. In 1559 William Cecil was suggesting the restoration of the unpopular Vagrancy Act of 1547 (see page 37). Furthermore he recommended that servants and labourers should not be allowed to leave their villages, and no one should be apprenticed unless his father was a gentleman or merchant, and owned land worth at least ten pounds a year.

iii) Assessment of Mid-Tudor Industry

The poor state of the industrial sector suggests that the Tudor economy had not advanced significantly by the 1550s. Slow progress in the heavy industries and fierce rivalry between the urban and rural manufacturers had helped to create a severe unemployment problem. Clearly there was insufficient job creation within the economy to absorb the surplus labour generated by a rising population. Consequently, no effective transfer of labour was taking place from the agricultural to the industrial sector. The situation was made worse by the down-turn in exports which created further unemployment in the textile trades.

5 The Mid-Tudor Trade Recession

> **KEY ISSUES** Why had English overseas trade become concentrated on Antwerp? To what extent was the mid-century trade recession caused more by political factors than economic considerations?

By the 1550s there was widespread destitution in the textile trades and in the towns. The long period of ever-rising cloth exports had ended, so bringing a sustained period of expansion from the 1460s to an abrupt halt. It is agreed that the basic cause of this problem was the decline of the Antwerp cloth market, but there were a number of contributory factors, all of which need to be considered to understand the economic difficulties in mid-Tudor England.

a) Long-term Causes

The underlying problem can be traced to developments in the fifteenth century. By the 1440s textile exports had risen to some 55,000 cloths a year, while wool exports had fallen to an annual 9,000 sacks. In the middle of the century trade was adversely affected by the general western European trade recession, following the population losses resulting from the Black Death and subsequent plague cycle. At the same time England was in a weak diplomatic position after defeat in the war with France and the beginning of the Wars of the Roses. Consequently, English merchants lost control of their markets in central Europe and the Baltic to their main commercial rivals, the German merchants of the Hanseatic League. When trade recovered in the 1460s, almost half the English cloth exports were controlled by the Hanse and other foreign merchants. At the same time the English share of the trade had become monopolised by the Merchant Adventurers, who were a powerful group of traders drawn mainly from the London Livery Companies. They owed their dominant position to the large loans which they gave to the Crown, in return for which they were granted privileges over other English merchants. Driven out of other continental markets, the Merchant Adventurers established themselves at Antwerp in the Netherlands.

This was to have a number of important consequences for English trade up to the 1550s. The Netherlands was a major centre for the dyeing and finishing of cloth, and this made it very convenient for the export of English 'white' textiles. Furthermore, at the time of the Merchant Adventurers' removal to Antwerp, the city was becoming the main commercial and financial centre in western Europe. This created what is known as the Antwerp-London 'funnel'. The monopoly of the Merchant Adventurers meant that English cloth exports came to be channelled through London, which controlled 90 per cent of the trade by the 1550s. At the same time English imports of wine, spices, manufactured goods and luxury items became concentrated on Antwerp. One beneficial effect of this commercial axis was that by the middle of the sixteenth century some 70 per cent of the country's overseas trade was controlled by English merchants. On the other hand, English ports such as Bristol, York, Hull and Southampton declined, and many merchants outside London complained that they were being excluded from the continental market.

b) Short-term Causes

The link with Antwerp created a variety of problems through its very success. Cloth exports had risen from some 40,000 cloths a year in the late fifteenth century, to 130,000 a year in the 1540s. At the same time exports of tin, leather and hides rose, and the volume of imports increased. Although this is considered to show notable economic growth, the market was not very stable. There were sudden slumps in demand, such as in the 1520s, which caused widespread unemployment in textile manufacturing areas. Much of the rise in the volume of exports in the 1540s was the result of the repeated debasement of the English coinage. This, by reducing the value of sterling against continental currencies, artificially stimulated demand for English goods abroad by making them cheaper, and so made the slump after 1550 even deeper. The importance of the trade to both England and the Netherlands made it a pawn in diplomatic exchanges and foreign policy. The early Tudors frequently used the threat of withholding cloth exports to try to force the Habsburg Empire into wars against France. Such a policy finally helped to bring about the decline of Antwerp when relationships with Charles V broke down during Northumberland's temporary alliance with France in 1550 (see page 66). Both sides placed restrictions on trade, and this forced English merchants to begin to look for new markets.

Although the Antwerp market did not finally collapse until the 1570s, its preceding decline left English trade in a very exposed position. During the first half of the sixteenth century the volume of exports to Antwerp had made English merchants disinclined to seek out alternative markets. In spite of advice, such as that given by Robert Thorne in his book *Declaration of the Indes* very little effort was made to establish new trade outlets within Europe, or elsewhere in the world. It was not until the initial slump in the trade to the Netherlands in the early 1550s that the Privy Council and the London merchants began to promote exploration in the search for new markets. The establishment of the Muscovy Company in 1553 (see page 68) was the first step in this direction. In any case, the underlying cause of the decline of the Antwerp market was the change in the pattern of demand. Both European and colonial buyers began to favour lighter types of fabric made of silk, cotton or linen mixed with wool, instead of the heavy woollen cloth of the 'old draperies'. This meant that during the second half of the sixteenth century English manufacturers not only had to find alternative markets, but, also, to restructure to meet the technical demands of the 'new draperies'.

c) Assessment of Mid-Tudor Trade

Clearly the concentration on trade with Antwerp had short-term benefits in terms of rising exports, but eventually proved temporarily disastrous for the English economy. In part, the situation was political, arising from England's reliance on Habsburg support in the wars with France. Fear of offending the Spanish Habsburgs meant that only limited attempts were made to break into their monopoly of world trade. The loss of Calais ended any lingering dreams of regaining a continental empire. Deteriorating relations between

England and Spain under Elizabeth I opened the way for a more vigorous search for markets outside Europe. This was to be the basis for expansion of world trade in the sevententh century.

6 Unemployment and Urban Recession

> **KEY ISSUES** What had caused many towns to be in such a depressed state by the 1550s? Why is it no longer thought that there was an 'urban crisis' in mid-Tudor England?

The levels of unemployment in the 1550s were made worse by what used to be called an 'urban crisis'. In some, but not all, respects this was considered to be a consequence of the development of the rural textile industry. The first stage of urban decline came from the effects of competition from the more cost-effective putting-out system. Then, in the fifteenth century, towns were adversely affected by the population losses caused by the Black Death and the continued influence of the plague cycle. Urban populations declined rapidly, especially because their crowded living conditions produced higher mortality rates. The situation was made worse because the fall in overall population drastically reduced the flow of migrants needed to maintain, or increase, the number of town dwellers. When population levels began to recover during the first half of the sixteenth century, the situation was reversed. Towns faced the problem of having to house, feed and employ large numbers of young and generally unskilled migrants from the countryside. At the same time, town guilds had to meet growing competition from the rural industries. It was this situation which forced early Tudor governments to try to legislate in favour of urban manufacturing.

Although the concept of an urban crisis is quite attractive – and many towns did suffer a severe decline – this can be regarded as part of the natural pattern of urban recession and recovery. While some towns went into temporary eclipse, others actually expanded. In any case, the picture is distorted by the abnormal expansion of London. Between 1500 and 1560 the population of London is estimated to have risen from 50,000 to 90,000. By comparison the population of Norwich, the second largest town, is thought to have remained virtually static at 12,000 over the same period. In part, this is a reflection of the influence of London's monopoly of the Antwerp trade. Possibly of equal importance was that London was becoming recognised as the centre of government and the capital of England. Although the rapid expansion of London did undoubtedly cast a temporary blight over many of the other towns, urban historians tend to see this as a positive development. London's emergence as a capital city is regarded as an engine for economic growth by the end of the sixteenth century.

7 Assessment of the Mid-Tudor Economy

> **KEY ISSUE** Despite its many problems, why is the mid-Tudor economy no longer thought to have been in crisis?

Although the mid-Tudor economy appeared to be in a weak state there is no clear evidence that it was in crisis. The agricultural sector was able to to feed the population except in bad harvest years. Heavy industry, while not dynamic, was in the process of restructuring. The expansion of exports and the rural textile industry was only halted by the slump in demand for the 'old draperies'. There is no real sign that rising unemployment was a key factor in the popular discontent in 1549. By the 1550s unemployment was becoming a problem in many towns, but most of the rural textile workers had other occupations and the produce of their cottage gardens to fall back on. This is not to say that there was not widespread hardship in many areas. However, it must be remembered that during the 1550s the level of population was actually falling, and this might account for the lack of discontent in spite of the run of very bad harvests.

It can be argued that the cause of any problems was more political than economic. The two mid-century decades were characterised by almost continuous warfare, which was the culmination of the wars started by Henry VIII in the 1520s. This protracted conflict disrupted the economies on both sides of the Channel. The situation was made worse by diplomatic manoeuvrings which artificially created slumps by stopping overseas trade. Possibly even more serious was the high cost of the wars. Debasements of the coinage helped to increase inflation and made goods and borrowing more expensive. Rising rents, prices and unemployment, along with static wages, curtailed demand among the bulk of the population. In turn, this acted as a decentive for people to invest in either agriculture or industry. Equally, the ruinously high levels of taxation from the 1520s were a further deterrent to investment. It is suggested that the cumulative effect of high taxation had, by the mid-century, seriously limited the cash reserves of all but the wealthiest landowners and merchants.

Even so, there was an underlying basic problem of a lack of investment and demand in the English economy. The rural elites are considered to have favoured building country mansions and buying luxury goods to maintain their life style rather than investing money to improve their estates. Similarly, the wealthy urban elites were more interested in improving their social position by purchasing country estates than expanding and improving their business interests. At the same time, there was still enough in-built self-sufficiency among the lower orders to limit any real consumer demand. This situation continued until the inflationary spiral ended in the 1650s. Until then landowners and industrialists were content to live off the profits generated by rising prices without making investments. After the 1650s it was necessary to invest in order to protect profit margins, and to benefit from growing consumer demand resulting from fuller employment, rising wages and expanding urban markets.

Working on Chapter 6

Your first step should be to familiarise yourself with the way historians study the Tudor economy. Your notes should set out the the various theories and approaches currently being used, and list the reasons why it is still thought that there might have been a mid-century economic crisis. You then need to note carefully why population levels had such a significant effect on the Tudor economy, and what problems were being caused by high population levels, particularly in 1549. You should then consider how well the agricultural sector was coping with the need to feed a rising poplation. Your next task is to note the varied levels of success being experienced in the mid-Tudor industrial sector. English overseas trade was suffering a number of problems at this time, and you need to note carefully the economic and non–economic reasons for this. Finally you need to decide how justified historians are in considering that the mid-Tudor economy was not in crisis.

Answering structured and essay questions on Chapter 6

This section will examine how to answer the long-term 'cause and effect' type of questions.

As is the case with social change, economic change is studied in the long-term. This means that any view of the mid-Tudor society and economy is just a snapshot isolated out of the broader perspective. So it is unlikely that you will ever be asked to write an entire essay on either social or economic change in the mid-century period. You are much more likely to be expected to discuss social and or economic change over a wider period, or to include social and economic factors within a general essay on the mid-century period. Only rarely will you be asked to combine social and economic issues in an answer restricted to the years 1547 to 1558. At the same time, you may well be asked what impact economic and social changes had upon political, diplomatic or religious issues.

1a) What effects had rising population levels had on the lower orders by 1550? *(12 marks)*
1b) What were the main causes of lower order unrest in 1549? *(18 marks)*

Question 1a) requires you to discuss the effects of unemployment, low wages, high rents, food shortages and inflation (which were direct results of population increase) on the living standards of the lower orders. Question 1b) is asking you to analyse the importance of the

Summary Diagram
A Crisis in the Economy?

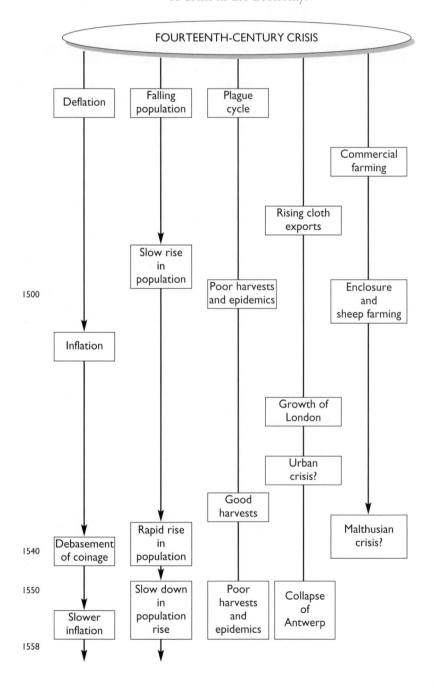

FOURTEENTH-CENTURY CRISIS

Deflation

Falling population

Plague cycle

Commercial farming

Rising cloth exports

Slow rise in population

Poor harvests and epidemics

Enclosure and sheep farming

1500

Inflation

Growth of London

Urban crisis?

Good harvests

Malthusian crisis?

1540   Debasement of coinage   Rapid rise in population

1550   Slower inflation   Slow down in population rise   Poor harvests and epidemics   Collapse of Antwerp

1558

same issues alongside other lower order grievances such as enclosure, or religious change, and to assess which were the main causes of the popular uprisings in 1549.

> What were the main causes of the decline in English exports abroad by 1558, and what effect was this having on the industrial sector?

The decline in overseas trade clearly had economic causes such as over-reliance on the sale of cloth, low levels of technology and the loss or decline of foreign markets. However, as part of your analysis you also have to consider the disruptive effect of wars, heavy taxation, diplomatic embargoes, English fear of offending Spain by breaking into world markets and the growing religious tensions. For the second part, while clearly the cloth industry was a major casualty, part of your analysis has to be a consideration of the industrial sector as a whole. In your conclusion you need state clearly what you consider to be the main causes of the declining volume of foreign exports, and to assess whether this decline was having an altogether adverse effect on English industries.

Source-based questions on Chapter 6

To answer these questions it is essential that you have a very firm grasp of the backgound and context of the documents. Remember that normally you are not only discussing the problem as perceived at the time. For example, in question 1d) you have to supply other causes and solutions.

1. Changes in Agriculture

Read the extract from Sir Thomas Smith's *A Discourse on the Commonweal of this Realm of England* (1549), given on pages 144-5. Answer the following questions:

a) What is the meaning of 'dearth' (line 5)? *(1 mark)*
b) What does the husbandman suggest were the incentives to enclose land? *(2 marks)*
c) What does the husbandman suggest was the reason why more land in his village was not enclosed? *(2 marks)*
d) What were the consequences of enclosure as reported by the husbandman? What other consequences of enclosure caused anxiety among the authorities at the time? *(6 marks)*
e) Who gained and who lost from sixteenth-century enclosures? *(4 marks)*

7 Conclusion: A Mid-Tudor Crisis?

POINTS TO CONSIDER

There no longer seems to be any significant support for the idea of there having been a crisis in any aspect of the mid-Tudor period. Identify the various reasons historians have for coming to this conclusion.

The concept of a mid-sixteenth-century crisis in England is now considered to be difficult to maintain. This is certainly true if by 'crisis' it is implied that the whole of the country, and all the people, were experiencing a crisis continuously between 1547 and 1558. Indeed, it is only really possible to say that the country as a whole and some sections of society underwent very short-lived crises at times between these dates. If this is the case, most historians would consider that this was normal for any country at any time. Mid-Tudor England faced a variety of problems. Many of these arose from the political, social and economic consequences of the political and economic breakdown at the end of the late Middle Ages. Others, like the reactions to the English Reformation, can be seen as very short-term. A few, such as the succession crisis of 1553, were responses to immediate events. At no time, even in 1549, was the country in danger of collapse, and for most people life went on as normal.

1 A Political Crisis?

KEY ISSUES Why has the concept of a mid-century political crisis now been largely discarded? How have the characters and abilities of Somerset, Northumberland and Mary Tudor been re-assessed? In what ways is recent research revealing more about political life under Edward and Mary?

Great importance has been attached to the potential constitutional and political crisis arising from Henry VIII's inability to provide an adult male heir. With the anarchy of the Wars of the Roses still very much a living memory there were obvious fears that the Tudor State would collapse into chaos. Such worries proved to be groundless. The permanent machinery of state continued to function without a break after 1547, showing that the overhaul of government under the first two Tudor monarchs had achieved a firm basis. At the same time the elites provided great support and loyalty to the legitimate monarchy. Although there was considerable rivalry between the political factions under Edward VI, it was no greater than it had been during the reign of Henry VIII. At no time, even in 1549 with the fall of Somerset, was there a real political crisis. The most dangerous moment came in 1553 with the death of Edward VI, when Northumberland tried to bar Princess Mary from the succession. Once again the elites were solid in their support for the legitimate descent, and the incident passed without crisis. It is true that the political leadership was often inept and indecisive between 1547 and 1558. Even so the structure of the administration continued to function without a check, and some useful measures of bureaucratic reform were passed. When Mary I died in 1558 the Crown was offered peacefully to her sister Elizabeth, a tribute to the strength of Tudor government.

Although there is general agreement that there was no serious mid-century political or constitutional crisis, opinions about the political leadership continue to vary. The 'good' Duke of Somerset is now seen in a much less favourable light, while the 'bad' Duke of Northumberland is credited with being a much more able politician than has traditionally been thought. Mary I is still regarded as a monarch without any real ability, but her reign is now thought to have achieved some significant advances. Speculation about the true nature of Mary's personality continues, and she is now regarded as having suffered in comparison with her more glamorous sister Elizabeth. At the same time, great interest continues to be shown in the nature of the ruling elites in general. Fresh analyses of the nobility and the gentry, both at national and county levels, are being produced. New works on the House of Lords and Stephen Gardiner throw more light on the workings of central government. Particular attention is being paid to the study of individual families and their circle of friends and associates, to reveal the part they played in local and central government. Such research continues to lead to a much greater understanding of the complex motives and ambitions behind the political factions of mid-Tudor England.

2 A Crisis in Foreign Affairs?

> **KEY ISSUES** Why is it considered that there was no real mid-century foreign policy crisis? Is it likely that even a dynamic English politician could have significantly changed the course of events? Why is it unlikely that new research will greatly modify the current views on foreign policy under Edward and Mary?

The lack of political leadership between 1547 and 1558 placed England in a weak diplomatic position. However, in no way did this amount to a crisis, as the country was never in real danger of foreign invasion. Moreover, it is unlikely that even strong leadership would have improved the diplomatic situation. Mid-century foreign policy was largely dictated by relatively long-term processes – the culmination of the Valois-Habsburg rivalry and the tactics of Henry VIII. Somerset and Northumberland inherited a war against France and Scotland which Henry VIII to all intents and purposes had already lost. Faced with an impossible military situation and a bankrupt Exchequer, Northumberland's decision to make an inglorious peace in 1550 was sensible. In any case, the evidence suggests that the Privy Council favoured peace to avoid any further economic problems. Mary I's deep Catholic convictions and her attachment to Philip II of Spain made it almost inevitable that she would support the Habsburgs in the final, indecisive stage of the Habsburg-Valois wars, which ended in 1558. The loss of Calais severed England's final link with the continent. When Elizabeth came to the throne she was faced with a completely different diplomatic situation.

Mid-Tudor foreign policy is still seen as being largely dictated by the broader aims of western European diplomacy which had dominated the first half of the sixteenth century. England's diplomatic position was further complicated by fears over the succession and religious reform. In the past, historians made considerable use of official papers and the correspondence between ambassadors and their courts to reconstruct events and policies. More recently they have begun to think that over-reliance on this type of evidence produced a one-sided view of the issues. Official documents only state what governments wish to be left on record, while the views of ambassadors like Renard (the accredited representative of the Holy Roman Empire in England) are bound to be partisan. For this reason, much greater attention is being paid to the correspondence and family papers of the many lesser diplomats involved in foreign affairs. These men were drawn from a wide range of families among the elites, and such research increases not only the understanding of the intricate nature of diplomacy, but, also, its relationship with domestic politics. However, it is still unlikely that historians will be able to probe much deeper than the official versions of the growing number of plots and intrigues with foreign powers, because families were very careful to destroy such incriminating evidence.

3 A Religious Crisis?

> **KEY ISSUES** Is it likely that if Mary had lived longer she would have succeeded in permanently restoring England to the Roman Catholic Church? How true is it to say that the reigns of Edward and Mary were marked by religious moderation and indifference rather than zeal? Why is it so difficult to assess the real religious views of the population?

It is difficult to assess the impact of religious reform because the English Reformation was too close for either its long or even short-term effects to be really felt by the middle of the century. Clearly religion had immediate consequences for politics and foreign policy, but in neither case can it be said to have caused a crisis. The longer-term influences of social and economic change were only to become apparent over the next century. It is now suggested that inclination of the bulk of the population were still towards Catholicism, and that, had Mary lived longer, England would have remained Roman Catholic. Certainly there was a great deal of religious compromise among the elites, and apathy, or even indifference, among the mass of the population towards religious change between 1547 and 1558. Zealous Catholics or Protestants were a small minority, and most people were prepared to tolerate the sudden switches of religious policy that occurred in the middle of the century. It seems likely that most people were content to follow the religion of their legitimate ruler. It is difficult to decide whether the religious uprising in the West Country was atypical. Possibly the western rebels, like their Norfolk counterparts, were indulging in nostalgia, and protesting for what they saw as better times in the past. Certainly the majority of the people of England were ready to accept the return of Protestantism under Elizabeth I.

There is still considerable disagreement about the true state of religion in mid-Tudor England. Although the course of religious change is well documented at the national level, it is still not clear whether Catholicism was maintaining, or Protestantism gaining, the support of the laity. While the loyalty of the Howard family for the Catholic faith, and the active patronage of Protestantism by the dowager Duchess of Suffolk are well documented, much less is known about the many uncommitted elite families. The growing volume of research into such families and their circle of friends is beginning to reveal more about the complexity of the motives governing political and religious alliances. It is a much greater problem to determine the attitudes of the ordinary people. A great deal of research is being carried out at county and parish level, but all this has revealed so far is that most people were prepared to conform by attending the services of the official religion. At present this is still being interpreted as showing apathy and indifference towards religion. However, many historians still consider that attendance at church merely shows that the lower orders were deferring to their superiors. What needs to be known, if that is ever possible, is how ordinary people actually felt about religion, and what form of religious devotion they followed in the privacy of their own homes.

4 A Crisis in Society?

KEY ISSUES How had the shape of feudal society changed by the 1550s? Why was the social structure still relatively stable in the 1550s? What areas of research are helping to provide a fuller picture of the lower orders?

The process of social change, although complicated and controversial, is easier to discern. Tentative models of social development since the end of the Middle Ages seem largely to conform to contemporary views of the shape of mid-Tudor society. Both the elites and the lower orders had been affected by change. Among the elites the emergence of the gentry from the ranks of the feudal aristocracy is still seen as a highly significant development. By the middle of the century the new structure had been strengthened by the sale of monastic and other church lands. Among the lower orders there had been considerable change over the same period. The servile, feudal peasantry had disappeared, to be replaced by a new hierarchy of yeomen, husbandmen, cottagers and labourers. Although a great gulf existed between the elites and the non-elites, the majority of the lower orders were freer and more prosperous than they had been 200 years before. There were already signs of increasing commercialism and competition at all levels of society. However, in the middle of the sixteenth century there still seems to have been considerable social stability, and little sign of social crisis. It was over the next century, when continued rising population added to social pressures, that real signs of tension within society began to emerge.

Although the actual process of structural change is relatively easy to discern, it is much harder to decide what was actually happening below the surface. Mid-sixteenth-century England was still an unruly nation, and violence was present at all levels of society. The government and the elites expected and feared outbreaks of popular rioting during the summer months as part of the normal course of events. These might be sparked off by village sports or quarrels between neighbours. A bad harvest, local enclosure, or unpopular taxation might cause more widespread disorder, as in 1549. Nevertheless, there appears to have been a considerable degree of co-operation between social groups, particularly at local levels. The growing number of county studies and the research into gentry and noble families is revealing the diverse motives governing social relationships among the elites, and their attitudes towards the lower orders. The lack of evidence makes it harder to investigate opinions among the non-elites. However, the official keeping of parish registers after 1538, and the growing number of wills and inventories left by people of relatively low social status helps historians to gain an insight into the lives of the ordinary people. Considerable attention continues to be given to the study of popular culture and disorder, and in particular to the family and the role of women in society.

5 An Economic Crisis?

> **KEY ISSUES** Why is it no longer thought that there was a mid-Tudor economic crisis? What were the basic problems with the domestic economy? How did the problem of the redeployment of surplus labour eventually solve itself?

Clearly the unsettled conditions of the two mid-century decades helped to depress the economy, and the outlook appeared very gloomy. Rising levels of unemployment, stagnation and destitution in many towns and the collapse of cloth exports would seem to indicate an economy on the verge of collapse. Yet it is no longer thought that the situation amounted to a crisis. Despite the disruptions caused by war, high taxation and debasements of the coinage, economic progress was maintained. Agriculture had become more efficient through enclosures, specialisation, and commercial farming. However, because of over-concentration on wool and other animal products, it was barely able to feed the increased population by 1550; a problem which was not to be fully overcome until the next century. There was a similar amount of change in the industrial sector. Heavy industry was still in the process of catching up with continental technology. The rural textile industry suffered temporary collapse in the 1550s after a century of expansion, but was already adapting to new demands by the second half of the century. The slump in the Antwerp cloth market in the 1550s had forced English merchants to begin to seek new markets in Europe, and to take an interest in world trade. The main difficulty was that the economy was unable to find employment for the surplus labour released from agriculture and created by a rising population.

Given the fragmentary and conflicting nature of the evidence, any conclusions on the mid-Tudor economy must be tentative. On-going research appears to confirm that the underlying problem, apart from the temporary loss of overseas markets, was a lack of investment and demand in the domestic economy. This situation was probably made worse by the high levels of taxation. In any case, while most people still lived in the countryside and had their own plots of land and access to common land they remained virtually self-sufficient. Rising prices further dampened demand, and this meant that the rural and urban elites had no incentive to invest to produce goods which they could not sell. However, as population levels rose there were no extra jobs in the smaller agriculture sector, and younger people had to find employment elsewhere. They travelled to the towns to seek work, which was often not available because of the lack of urban investment. This was the situation that caused the serious problems in towns in the 1550s, and created the friction between urban and rural industries. Yet, this seemingly insoluble impasse contained its own solution. Because of high urban mortality rates towns needed migrants from the countryside in order to expand. As the numbers of migrants increased towns had to invest in order to house, feed and employ them. This process was led by the rapid growth of London which benefited from being the national capital and major port. As the towns were dependent on the countryside for supplies, the urban food markets created demand, which encouraged neighbouring landowners to begin to invest in their estates. When the inflationary spiral ended in the 1650s, no landowner or industrialist could just rely on rising prices to provide their profits, and so levels of investment increased. At the same time, domestic demand rose because of fuller employment, higher wages and lower prices, so beginning a benign cycle of economic growth.

6 1549 – A Year of Crisis?

KEY ISSUES What combination of circumstances created particular problems in 1549? If even the events of 1549 cannot be seen as a crisis, what does this tell us about the stability of the English State?

If there was a crisis in the mid-sixteenth century it was in 1549, and was created by a range of misfortunes. There was a weak, insolvent government, over-stretching its resources by trying to fight a war on two fronts. Moreover, the government was attempting to introduce drastic religious reforms. It also aroused the hostility of the elites and non-elites by its social and economic policies.

By 1549 the population, which had been rising rapidly for the last decade, was peaking at around 3 million. Prices, fuelled by currency debasements and increasing population levels, had doubled since the beginning of the century. A run of good growing seasons was brought to an end by a wet summer, and the harvest in 1549 was poor. This came at a time when agriculture was already struggling to feed the higher level of population, and so grain prices rose. Under these circumstances it is not surprising that underlying discontent came to the surface in the form of popular rebellions. Even so, if Somerset had not been unwilling to withdraw troops from Scotland and France, and if there had not been a power struggle developing in the Privy Council, it is unlikely that the situation would have got out of hand. Once the government had mobilised sufficient troops, the rebellions were suppressed with comparative ease. It must be considered that, if this was the worst that could happen in a particularly bad year, there is little reason to see the mid-century as a period of crisis.

Working on Chapter 7

This chapter reconsiders the issues raised in Chapter 1, and in particular assesses the issue of whether there was a mid-Tudor crisis. At the same time, it examines the changing attitudes among historians towards the concept of crises, and reviews some of the major trends of historical research into this period. You must think carefully about whether the idea of a mid-century crisis is useful in interpreting this period of Tudor history. Your notes should set out the arguments for and against a crisis, and indicate the direction of current historical research. Use the questions posed in the issues boxes to help structure your notes

Answering structured and essay questions on Chapter 7

Examiners are likely to set a variety of 'synoptic' questions. Such questions are designed to test either your ability to handle one particular theme over a long time period, or a number of themes in relation to one issue over a shorter time period. Think about this two-part question.

1a) How great a danger were the popular uprisings to the government in 1549? *(10 marks)*

1b) Why is the mid-sixteenth century no longer considered to have been a period of crisis for the Tudors? *(20 marks)*

Question a) is a straightforward 'how far/to what extent?' type of question in which the central point you need to consider is whether the government was ever in a real danger of falling because of the uprisings. Question b) is a synoptic question of the second type. To answer the question you should point out that it was once thought that there were possible crises in politics, foreign policy, religion, society and the economy. You need to write one or two paragraphs on each of these topic to indicate why they are no longer thought to have been a source of crisis, and then sum up your argument in a conclusion.

Now consider the two questions below.

How great an influence did religion have during the Tudor period?
Did rebellions ever pose a serious threat to the Tudors?

Although outside the scope of this book, these are examples of the other type of synoptic question you are likely to encounter. Indeed, depending on the type of course you are studying, they might cover an even longer time-span. You have to be careful in structuring your answer to such questions because of the amount and diversity of the material that you are expected to handle. For this reason, the introduction and conclusion in answers to this type of question are of crucial importance.

For the first example your introduction must outline the scope of you answer and put it into a wide context. You are expected to assess the effect of religious change on politics, foreign policy, society and the economy, but at the same time you are considering what actual impact it had on the population in general. In the main body of the essay you should very briefly outline the five main points of religious developments between 1485 to 1603 – tensions with the Papacy, the influence of Lollardy, Humanism and Luther (the background to the Reformation); the break with Rome, the Pilgrimage of Grace and the dissolution of the monasteries (the first political Reformation); the swing towards extreme Protestantism (influence of Calvin) and popular uprisings (the second political Reformation); the swing back to Roman Catholicism under Mary; and finally the attempt to maintain unity of belief under the Elizabethan Church (the third political Reformation). Then you must devote one or two paragraphs each to assessing the political, diplomatic, social and economic outcomes of the changes. Then in your conclusion you need to assess their overall impact of religion, and finally consider whether or not most English people really cared about religion or just conformed to the religion of whoever was in power at the time.

The second question is not quite as wide-ranging as the first one, but it needs equally careful handling. Again, your introduction must outline the scope of your answer, this time by indictating which rebellions you are going to discuss, and the reasons why you chose them. It might be a good idea choose one rebellion from each reign: for example, the Cornish Rebellion of 1497, the Pilgrimage of Grace of 1536, Kett's Rebellion of 1549, Wyatt's Rebellion of 1553 and the Northern Rebellion of 1569. This would help you to illustrate the range of grievances that caused rebellions and the varied threats they posed to each government. In the main part of your essay you should deal with each rebellion in turn by outlining the main course of events and assessing how great a threat it was to the government of the time. Finally, the conclusion should assess the extent to which the Tudor regimes were ever under threat from rebellions.

Further Reading

A great variety of books have been written about Tudor England, including some specifically on the mid-century period. Although you only have a relatively limited amount of time for additional reading, you should not be content to read general histories of the period, however good they are. You should also try to look at some of the more specialist volumes. The following suggestions are representative of the different types of books available, and they have been selected because they are both readable and will give you the flavour of the range of interpretations of the period.

J. Guy, *Tudor England* (OUP Paperback, 1990).
P. Williams, *The Later Tudors: England, 1547-1603* (OUP, 1995).
J. Lotherington, ed., *The Tudor Years* (Hodder & Stoughton, 1994).
These are the most recent and accessible general histories and they will give you an insight into the latest research on and interpretation of the Tudor period. They also contain useful chapters on the economy and society.

J. Loach, *A mid-Tudor crisis?* (Historical Association pamphlet, 1992).
D.M. Loades, *The Mid-Tudor Crisis, 1545-65* (Macmillan, 1992).
These are the latest and most readable assessments of the mid-Tudor crisis, and they are particularly useful in highlighting the reassessments and changing interpretations of the period.

D.M. Loades, *The Reign of Mary Tudor: Politics, Government and Religion in England, 1553-1558* (2nd. Ed., Longman, 1991).
D.M. Loades, *The Reign of Edward VI* (Headstart History, 1994).
R. Titler, *The Reign of Mary I* (2nd edn., Longman, 1991).
R.K. Marshall, *Mary I* (HMSO pamplet, 1993).
These books give some very useful insights into how the assessment of the reigns of Edward VI and Mary I continues to change.

J. Youings, *Sixteenth Century England* (Penguin Books, 1984).
This continues to be the most readable introduction to Tudor society.

D.C. Coleman, *The Economy of England, 1450-1750* (OUP, 1977).
This is still the most readable book on the English economy. It gives a clear and uncomplicated explanation of the economy, and has many useful tables and graphs.

D.M. Pallister, *The Age of Elizabeth: England under the Later Tudors 1547-1603* (2nd edn., Longman, 1992).
Apart from a valuable section on the economy between 1547 and 1558, this book also has many useful tables and graphs.

N. Heard, *Tudor Economy and Society* (Hodder & Stoughton, 1992).

This Access to History volume puts mid-Tudor social and economic problems into a wider context.

I. Wallerstein, *The Modern World System 1* (Academic Press, 1974).
For a very readable insight into the theoretical background and the key debates on the period this book is still invaluable. There are very good sections on the medieval background, economic crises and the growth of commercialism, the rise of the State, and on the debate about the rise of the gentry.

Sources on Mid-Tudor England

There is a good range of accessible published primary material which includes coverage of the period 1547-58.

G.R. Elton, *The Tudor Constitution* (2nd edn., CUP, 1982).
This book is still the standard volume for constitutional and governmental papers.

D. Cook, *Sixteenth Century England 1450-1600* (Macmillan, reprinted 1989)
The documentary sections on the period 1547-58 are very useful.

M. Levine, *Tudor Dynastic Problems, 1467-1571* (George Allen and Unwin, 1973).
This volume has a rather different selection of documents, and is particularly useful in gaining an insight into the problems of the Tudor succession.

A. Fletcher and D. MacCulloch, *Tudor Rebellions* (4th edn., Longman, 1997).
This thoroughly revised edition contains good coverage of the rebellions of 1549 from primary sources, and some useful analysis.

W.T. Sheils, *The English Reformation, 1530-1570* (Longman, 1989).
This seminar book discusses recent interpretations of religious change and has a good documentary section.

H.E.S. Fisher and A.R.J. Jurica, *Documents in English Economic History from 1000-1760* (Bell and Sons, 1977).
This is now the standard source for economic documents.

J.M. Jack, *Trade and Industry in Tudor and Stuart England* (George Allen and Unwin, 1977).
This seminar book contains some useful discussion of approaches to economic history, and provides a range of alternative documentary sources.

Index